PRAISE FOR RICHARD LEDERER

"Richard Lederer has done it again — another delightful, witty, and hugely absorbing celebration of the English language. Is there no stopping this man?" -Bill Bryson, author of *The Mother Tongue*

"Richard Lederer is to wordplay what John Philip Sousa is to marches." -Rod L. Evans, author of *Tyrannosaurus Lex*

"Richard Lederer is the true King of Language Comedy." -Sidney Sheldon, author of *Master of the Game*

"Richard Lederer ought to be declared a national treasure. No one has more fun with the English language." -*Richmond Times Dispatch*

"Columnist Extraordinaire." -*The New Yorker*

"Lederer beguiles and bedazzles." -*Los Angeles Times*

"If you love words, you will love Richard Lederer." -*The Dallas Morning News*

"America's Top Pun." -*Chicago Tribune*

"It's a wonder that anyone learns to speak English. It's such a complicated language. Your reward for learning, though, is to be transported to the wonderful world of word play. You couldn't have a better guide to that world than Richard Lederer. You'll have fun, and when you're done, you'll have discovered aspects of English you never thought about before. Hang on to your hat. You're not in Kansas anymore." -Caroline McCullagh, author of *Quest for the Ivory Caribou*

"Wordplay that's fast, furious, and funny." -puzzle master Will Shortz

LEDERER'S LANGUAGE & LAUGHTER

RICHARD LEDERER

Waterside Productions

ISBN-13: 978-1-958848-38-8 print edition
ISBN-13: 978-1-958848-39-5 e-book edition

Waterside Productions

2055 Oxford Ave
Cardiff, CA 92007
www.waterside.com

to Stu, Harvey, Lee, Bo, Stan, and Cherri,
who made the world a happier place as they passed through

CONTENTS

Introduction:
They Who Laugh, Last

A thousand thanks to you, my fellow verbivores, logophiles, and wordaholics, for your warm reception of my words about words in my shelves-full of books. But when I look up the meaning of *warm* in my dictionary, I find the definition is "not so hot."

I try hard to be a model author. Alas, though, my dictionary defines *model* as "a small imitation of the original." But I'm not an imitation; I am an original — and I try to tell the blunt truth about language. When I turn to my dictionary for support, I find that *blunt* is defined as "not sharp."

Many of my readers tell me that nothing is better than my books. I'm flattered until I realize that such a statement can mean reading no book at all is preferable to reading my scribblings.

I know these things because I am an unrepentant English major. In 1955, I entered Haverford College (our motto is "We haven't heard of you either") as a pre-med student aiming to major in Chemistry, but I soon found that I was reading the chemical formulas for their literary value. I realized that something was wrong; so, at the eleventh hour, I switched to English as my area of concentration. Ever since, I have earned my bread as an English major.

You know the jokes:

- What do you say to an English major after graduation? "I'll have fries with that burger."
- Good news for English majors: They're raising the minimum wage.
- What's the difference between a bird and an English major? A bird can make a deposit on a car.
- Don't laugh derisively at us English majors, or we'll squirt less foam on your lattes.

People call me a walking dictionary. I thought they meant I was smart with a big vocabulary, but, apparently, they think I'm just thick. Building a strong vocabulary is important in life, so today I'm teaching you the word *plethora*. I hope it means a lot to you. I'm less in love with the word *dearth*. It means very little to me.

In truth, *Lederer's Language & Laughter* is actually good for you. The President's Council on Humor Fitness requires me to state that the information and humor served up in these pages are certified fast acting. The active ingredients are pure, fat-free, and contain no artificial sweeteners or preservatives. I've also coated the covers with epoxy and included a chapter about anti-gravity so that you literally will not be able to put this book down.

My book is also guaranteed gluten-free, even though, with more than 50 books under my belt, I'm a glutton for publishment. Recently, our home telephone rang, and my wife Simone picked up the call. The voice at the other end asked, "Is Richard Lederer there?"

Simone said, "Yes Rich is here, but he's writing a book."

"That's okay," said the caller. "I'll just hang on here until he's done."

The only side effects of ingesting the contents of this tome are laughter and learning. This book is unconditionally guaranteed to supply the recommended daily allowance of chuckles, chortles, cackles, grins, giggles, guffaws, and verbal fiber. This book is so cool that it requires no refrigeration and never expires.

Turns out that laughter can be hazardous to illness. In *Make 'Em Laugh,* William Fry explains, "When laughter gets to the point where it is convulsive, almost every muscle in the body is involved." A belly-shaking guffaw stimulates circulation; tones the muscles, energizes the lungs, excites endorphins, adds T cells to the immune system, reduces pain, inflammation, and muscle tension, boosts the neuro-transmitters needed for alertness and memory, stabilizes blood sugar levels, increases motivation to learn, provides superb aerobic exercise — well, you get the idea. They who laugh, last.

I myself try to stay mentally and physically fit.

I get plenty of exercise racking my brain, wrestling with details, grappling with problems, plowing through paperwork, trotting out proposals, slinging the bull, jumping to conclusions, hopping on the bandwagon, bucking the system, stretching the truth, skating on thin ice, bending the rules, breaking promises, splitting hairs, stirring up trouble, running my mouth, flying off the handle, poking fun, pushing my luck, pulling rank, jogging my memory, climbing the corporate ladder, twisting someone's arm, carrying things too far, passing the buck, dodging responsibility, skipping lunch, punching the clock, and exercising my prerogative.

I also try to keep my nose to the grindstone, my shoulder to the wheel, my hand on the tiller, my foot on the gas, my ear to the ground, my face to the wind, and my eye on the ball. Then I go see my chiropractor,

Laughter is also an elixir for the mind. Tests administered before and after humor therapy reveal a reduction of stress and depression and a heightened sense of well-being and creativity.

More and more, science is discovering that it hurts only when we *don't* laugh.

"Laughter is to life what shock absorbers are to automobiles. It won't take the potholes out of the road, but it sure makes the ride smoother," avows Barbara Johnson. Pressing into service another simile, she adds, "Laughter is like changing a baby's diaper: It doesn't permanently solve problems, but it makes things more tolerable for a while."

So, go forth and practice random acts of laughter, and remember, one of those acts should be to laugh at yourself. If you can do that, you'll never cease to be amused.

Richard Lederer
richardhlederer@gmail.com
www.verbivore.com

Funny Bone

"I'm pretty sure
I'm a Type O"

BEST LANGUAGE LAUGH LINES

The source of that tingly sensation you feel when you strike your arm is the knob on the end of the bone running from the shoulder to the elbow. The medical name for that bone is the *humerus,* and back in 1840, some clever wag seized upon the homophonic similarity of *humerus* and *humorous* and dubbed the humerus the *funny bone,* a learned pun that has become part of our language. Since then, we've found out that if you boil a funny bone, it becomes a humerus laughing stock.

To thrive in life, you need three bones: a wishbone, a backbone, and a funny bone. This section of *Lederer's Language & Laughter* is designed to tickle your humerus.

Language is like the air we breathe. It's invisible, inescapable, and indispensable, and we take it for granted. But when we take the time to step back and listen to the sounds that escape from the holes in people's faces and to explore the paradoxes and vagaries of English, we find that hot dogs can be cold, darkrooms can be lit, homework can be done in school, nightmares can take place in broad daylight while morning sickness and daydreaming can take place at night, tomboys are girls and midwives can be men, hours — especially happy hours and rush hours — often last longer than 60 minutes, quicksand works *very* slowly, boxing rings are square, and silverware and glasses can be made of plastic and tablecloths of paper.

Has it occurred to you that most bathrooms don't have any baths in them. In fact, a dog can go to the bathroom under a tree — no bath, no room; it's still going to the bathroom. And doesn't it seem a little bizarre that we go to the bathroom in order to go to the bathroom?

Because language is naturally playful, we human beings love to make jokes about words. Here are my favorite linguistic tours de farce:

- Shouldn't hemorrhoids be called asteroids?
- Every time you make a typo, the errorists win.
- Is there a word that uses all the vowels, including *y*? Unquestionably.
- Do you know that the word *gullible* is not in the dictionary?
- The only place where *success* comes before *work* is in the dictionary.
- I hate it when people use big words just to make themselves sound perspicacious.
- It's better to be optimistic than misty optic.
- Your knowledge of American history isn't vast. It's half vast.
- Did you hear about the cat who swallowed some cheese? She sat by a mousehole and waited with baited breath.
- Did you hear about the dyslexic, agnostic insomniac? She stayed up all night tossing and turning, wondering if there was a dog. She could turn lemons into lemonade — but she could also turn *lemons* into *melons*. (Think about that one.)
- Did you hear about the Buddhist who, when he was sitting in a dentist's chair, never asked for Novocain? He was able to transcend dental medication.
- Don't sweat the petty things, and don't pet the sweaty things.
- It is better to leave the house and kiss your wife good-bye than to leave your wife and kiss the house good-bye.
- A linguistics professor was lecturing to her class one day. "In English," she proclaimed, "a double negative forms a positive. In some languages though, such as Russian and Spanish, a double negative is still a negative. However, there is no language in which a double positive can form a negative."

A voice from the back of the room piped up, "Yeah, right."

- Writer and dictionary maker Samuel Johnson was once told, "You smell!"

  "No," Doctor Johnson corrected his accuser. "*You* smell. *I* stink!"

- In a variation of that story, Dr. Johnson was dandling a chambermaid on his knee. Johnson's wife entered the scene and exclaimed, "Samuel, I am surprised!"

  "No, my dear," Johnson explained, "*I* am surprised. *You* are astonished!"

- Some contend that there is no difference between the words *complete* and *finished*. But there clearly is. When you marry the right woman, you are complete. If you marry the wrong woman, you are finished. And, if the right one catches you with the wrong one, you are completely finished.

- Perhaps you wonder how my wife, Simone, puts up with living with a compulsive punster. Well, the other day, I said to her, "Did you hear my last pun?"

  She replied, "I sure hope so!" A little later, she said she missed me. That sounded like a good thing, but she was reloading.

- How do you describe a person who speaks three languages? Trilingual.

  How do you describe a person who speaks two languages? Bilingual.

  And how do you describe a person who speaks one language? American.

- The most renowned scientists of all time were invited to be honored at the White House. Pierre and Marie Curie radiated enthusiasm. Boyle said he was under too much pressure. Franklin told the hosts to go fly a kite. Heisenberg was uncertain if he could make it. Hawking said he'd try to string enough time together to make a space in his schedule. Archimedes was buoyant about the opportunity. Sagan had billions and billions of other things to do. Pavlov drooled at the thought. Watson and Crick accepted, on the condition that the dance band played the twist. Schrodinger had to take his cat to the vet, or did he?

- What do you call a super-articulate dinosaur? A thesaurus.
- I bought the world's worst thesaurus yesterday. "How bad is it?" you ask. Not only is it awful. It's awful.
- What does a thesaurus eat for breakfast? Synonym buns, just like the ones grammar used to bake.
- I used to be poor. Then I bought a thesaurus. Now I'm impecunious.
- I love using a thesaurus because a mind is a terrible thing to garbage.
- I recently asked my horse if she had stolen my thesaurus. She replied, "Neigh, no, nah, negative, negatory, never, nope, not on your life, no way."
- I regret to inform you that yesterday, a senior editor of *Roget's Thesaurus* assumed room temperature, bit the dust, bought the farm, breathed his last, came to the end of the road, cashed in his chips, called it quits, checked out, cooled off, croaked, deep sixed, departed this life, expired, finished out the row, flatlined, gave up the ghost, headed for the hearse, headed for the last roundup, kicked off, kicked the bucket, lay down one last time, lay with the lilies, left this mortal plane, met the Grim Reaper, his maker, and Mr. Jordan, passed away, passed on, pegged out, perished, permanently changed his address, pulled the plug, pushed up daisies, rested in peace, rested under the sod, rang the knell, slipped his cable, shuffled off his mortal coil, sprouted wings, took a dirt nap, took the long count, traveled to kingdom come, turned up his toes, went kaput, west, the way of all flesh, belly up, to glory, across the creek, to the happy hunting grounds and his final reward — and, of course, he died.

Here's some fun with letter play — making the alphabet dance:

- *Boss* is spelled that way because your boss is a backward double *s-o-b*.
- I don't play golf because the word *golf* is *flog* spelled backward, and I don't want to flog myself in an effort to be subpar.
- When you're feel *stressed*, just reverse those letters and treat yourself to *desserts*.
- Why do we pay so much of our hard-earned money to the government? Because the letters in *THE IRS* spell *THEIRS*.
- When a boy and a girl are *amiable together*, he may wonder, *am I able to get her?*

ONCE UPON A RHYME TIME

We usually think of rhyme as a musical device found only in poems and songs, but, in fact, rhyme is the name of the game. Rhyme appeals so powerfully to the human ear that, if we listen carefully, we can discover a surprising number of common, everyday words and phrases that contain rhyme. Let's sneak a peek at the saga of Henny Penny.

Once upon a rhyme time, Henny Penny got the heebie-jeebies that the sky was falling. Figuring that, with her mojo, it's use it or lose it, she dashed pell-mell, helter-skelter, hither and thither, higgledy-piggledy, hugger-mugger, willy-nilly, balls to the wall, and here, there, and everywhere, shouting, "Yoo-hoo! May Day! You snooze; you lose! This isn't sci-fi! It's the real deal for double trouble! The sky is falling!"

Keeping her eyes on the prize, Henny Penny came upon roly-poly, jelly-bellied Chicken Licken, no longer in his heyday. Licken huffed and puffed at Henny Penny, "Tee-hee, I don't want to create ill will with a blame game, but what's all this hubbub and hurly burly about? Your whale of a tale sounds like a lot of phony baloney, folderol, razzmatazz, claptrap, and mumbo jumbo to me. I don't believe in abracadabra and hocus-pocus voodoo, and I don't want to kowtow to a shock jock with a hodgepodge of pie in the sky."

"Jeepers creepers and geez Louise! That's a low blow with a blackjack," clucked Henny Penny, who was left high and dry with her spirit at half-staff. "It's not easy-peasy trying to do my fair share by being fair and square to all those near and dear to me. Why are you making such a to-do, taking potshots, and calling my story a rinky-dink hunk of junk? I'm no Humpty-Dumpty crumb bum. I may cry 'boo-hoo,' but I'm not a rum-dum hobo panhandling with a squeegee for freebees. Sticks and stones may break my bones, but names will never make or break me."

Backtracking, Henny Penny went off looking for Cocky Locky to tell him that the sky was falling. But Locky was too busy being a crackerjack hotshot and a hoity-toity wheeler-dealer out and about downtown to wine and dine bigwigs, throw funny money at jet-set fat cats with big paydays, and hobnob with dressed-for-success rich bitches at fancy-schmantzy wingdings.

Feeling the wear and tear of walking a fine line through a stress test, off Henny Penny scurried to hippy-dippy Loosey Goosey. "Whadaya know, Daddy-o?" honked Goosey. "Don't be a namby-pamby. Take a chill pill, go with the flow, and party hearty. I've got a razzle-dazzle, killer-diller, no-fuss-no-muss idea that's the bee's knees and will float your boat, flick your Bic, and knock your socks off. I'm hot to trot, so let's get down to the nitty-gritty and hustle our bustle to a spring fling attended by artsy-fartsy Deadheads who meet and greet, have tons of fun in the sun, and feel their flower power while smoking mellow yellow wacky tobacky. With fans wearing their backpacks, tie-dyed shirts, and zoot suits, it'll be a real blast from the past.

"It'll be better than a prime-time chick flick on the boob tube, a sure cure for all your gloom and doom. I'll get palsy-walsy and make hanky-panky with hotsy-totsy, lovey-dovey tootsie-wootsies who get sky-high ready to do handstands on the grandstands and the bandstand.

"Then we'll dance the hootchy-kootchy, boogie-woogie, hokey pokey, and funky monkey. Be there or be square! We'll be made in the shade and in like Flynn! If you want to be a fuddy-duddy no-show, then I'll see you later, alligator."

"After a while, crocodile, but not while the sky is falling," replied Henny Penny, and she put the pedal to the metal to waylay her friend herky-jerky Turkey Lurkey. But plug-ugly Lurkey wasn't any help either. In fact, he was more harum-scarum than Loosey

Goosey, acting like a Silly Billy bozo, a run-and-gun local yokel hillbilly pogo sticking around like a nitwit, a lamebrain who was drunk as a skunk with a peg leg. "What can one teeny-weeny, itsy-bitsy piece of sky falling down matter?" gobbled Lurkey like a ding-a-ling eager beaver trying to play a solo on an oboe and a hurdy-gurdy at the same time.

With ants in her pants, Henny Penny decided that her court of last resort was to get back on track by consulting fuzzy-wuzzy Foxy Loxy. Licken was sick of the humdrum, ragtag hoi polloi and their honky-tonk ways, while Loxy's claim to fame was that he was a true-blue guru.

"Okey dokey, you lucky duck," said Foxy Loxy with a tutti-frutti smile. "Your goof-proof, rough-and-tough, rock'em sock'em story beats the heat, takes the cake, and fills the bill by hook and by crook, lock, stock, and barrel. Let's go to my teepee for a powwow and a chalk talk." So off the two ran to Loxy's den, where Loxy began to speed-read his handy-dandy cookbook about slicing and dicing sweetmeat and chugalugging it down with Mai Tais, Tia Marias, pale ale, and near beer.

At this, Henny Penny sensed double trouble and yelled, "Ah-ha! Oho! Who says that might makes right? I'm not one of your meals on wheels, you big pig! Never ever! Now it's a no go! It's one and done!"

"Holy moly and hell's bells, Peewee," snarled Loxy, looking less and less like a Care Bear and more and more like a lean, mean eating machine. "You're cruisin' for a bruisin', your ass is grass, and you are screwed, blued, and tattooed. That seals the deal! It's my way or the highway!"

"Don't have a shit fit, Loxy! This cave could really use a sump pump and a pooper-scooper, you unsanitary bowwow! No way, José, and up your nose with a rubber hose!" shot back Henny Penny, as she beat a retreat.

Then wham, bam, thank you, ma'am. The sky fell down and killed them all, proving that sticks and stones can break one's bones, haste makes waste, and well begun is only half done.

The Art of Inventive Invective

Sigmund Freud declared, "The first human being who hurled a curse instead of a spear was the founder of civilization." Through the centuries, we humans have exercised our highest powers of linguistic license and verbal vituperation by hurling incandescently inventive invective at each other:

I've had a perfectly wonderful evening. But this wasn't it. *-Groucho Marx*

His mother should have thrown him away and kept the stork. *-Mae West*

Katharine Hepburn's performance ran the gamut of emotions, from A to B. *-Dorothy Parker*

He has delusions of adequacy. *-Walter Kerr*

He has van Gogh's ear for music. *-Billy Wilder*

Women who want to be equal with men lack ambition. *-Timothy Leary*

A woman without a man is like a fish without a bicycle. *-Irina Dunn*

Whatever women must do, they must do twice as well as men to be thought half as good. Luckily, this is not difficult. *-Charlotte Whitton*

Groucho Marx once wrote to a novelist, "From the moment I received your book, I was convulsed with laughter. Someday I intend to read it." Authors are especially adept at skewering other authors:

Truman Capote on Jack Kerouac's work: "That's not writing! That's typing!"

Mary McCarthy on Lillian HHHellman: "Every word she writes is a lie, including *and* and *the*."

Ruth Rendell on Agatha Christie: "To say that Agatha Christie's characters are cardboard cut-outs is an insult to cardboard cut-outs."

William Faulkner on Ernest Hemingway: "He has never been known to use a word that might send a reader to the dictionary."

Ernest Hemingway on William Faulkner: "Poor Faulkner. Does he really think big emotions come from big words?"

If you're like me, you have, from time to time, encountered a situation that cried out for a snappy verbal comeback. But the comeback flashed in your mind a few minutes to a few hours too late and you could only sigh wistfully, "I wish I'd thought of that line then." There's actually a name in French for that feeling: *esprit d'lescalier,* "the wit of the staircase." The conjured image is of you, having ascended the staircase on your way to bed, long after the opportunity for a retort has passed, thinking of the perfect answer.

One quality that marks many great men and women in politics and the arts is their ability to marshal language on the spot. Rather than pausing on the staircase minutes or hours after the juicy encounter, these luminaries respond instantly with the perfect rapier-like riposte that leaves their antagonists glassy-eyed with astonishment or embarrassment.

Some collectors of verbal wit consider an exchange between Winston Churchill and George Bernard Shaw to be unsurpassed. Churchill and Shaw were among the most brilliant men of their time but inhabited opposite ends of the political spectrum. One day, Shaw sent Churchill an invitation that read, "Dear Mr. Churchill: Enclosed please find two tickets for the opening night of my play *Major Barbara.* Please bring a friend — if you have one."

Replied Churchill, "My Dear GBS: I thank you very much for the invitation and tickets. Unfortunately, I am otherwise engaged on that night, but could I have tickets for the second night — if there is one?"

Women have contributed their fair share of verbal payback. Writer, critic, and humorist Dorothy Parker and playwright, journalist, and politician Clare Boothe Luce engaged in a long-running feud. The two brilliant women once arrived simultaneously at a narrow doorway.

"Age before beauty," said Mrs. Luce, stepping aside.

"Pearls before swine," purred Parker as she glided through the doorway.

When a socialite told actress and novelist Ilka Chase, "I enjoyed reading your book. Who wrote it for you?" Chase quickly struck back with "Darling, I'm so glad that you liked it. Who read it to you?"

A Member of Parliament confronted Prime Minster Benjamin Disraeli with "Sir, you will either die on the gallows or of some unspeakable disease."

"That depends, sir," said Disraeli, "on whether I embrace your policies or your mistress."

At a gathering, Noel Coward teased fellow writer Edna Ferber for wearing a tailored suit, "You look almost like a man."

She shot back, "So do you."

Pacifist Mahatma Gandhi was asked, "What do you think of Western civilization?"

Gandhi observed, "I think it would be a good idea."

Having begun this parade of resourceful repartee with Sir Winston Churchill, I choose to end the extravaganza with this zinger: At a weekend party, Churchill found himself seated next to Lady Nancy Astor, a longtime political foe who had fought him in House of Commons debates.

When coffee was served, the acid-tongued Nancy hissed, "Sir Winston, if I were your wife, I would put poison in your coffee."

"Nancy," the great man growled. "If I were your husband, I would drink it!"

Famous Last Words

As William Shakespeare noted in his tragedy *Hamlet,* "All that lives must die passing through nature to eternity." As they shuffle off their mortal coil and exit the earthly stage, some men and women have delivered famous last words, curtain lines that are strikingly memorable for the life that pulses through them, deathly prose possesses a deep plot of grave humor:

When his doctor informed him that his condition was terminal, Henry John Temple Palmerston, British prime minster, exclaimed, "Die, my dear doctor? That's the last thing I will do!"

When Bob Hope, on his deathbed at the age of one hundred, was asked where he wanted to be buried, he responded, "Surprise me."

Comedian W.C. Fields uttered these final words: "On the whole, I'd rather be in Philadelphia."

German poet Heinrich Heine assured his family, "God will pardon me. It's His profession."

German philosopher Wilhelm Hegel's final observation was "Only one man understood me — and he didn't understand me."

As writer Gertrude Stein was closing the final chapter of her life, she murmured to her life partner Alice B. Toklas, "What is the answer?" When Toklas did not respond, Stein then asked, "In that case, what is the question?"

Welsh poet Dylan Thomas, who put the quart before the hearse by drinking himself to death, slurred, "I've had 18 straight whiskeys. I think this is a record."

In contrast are the last words of James Croll, teetotaling Scots physicist: "I'll take a wee drop o' that. I don't think there's much fear o' me learnin' to drink now."

Some people insist on remaining unstintingly professional up to the very end:

Ever the showman, Florenz Ziegfeld Jr. enthused, "Curtain! Fast music! Lights! Ready for the last finale! Great! The show looks good, the show looks good!"

The noted English surgeon Joseph Henry Green looked at his doctor, pointed to his heart, and diagnosed, "Congestion." Then he took his own pulse and said, "Stopped," and expired.

Lawrence, a third-century deacon who was later sainted by the Catholic Church, was roasted alive on orders by the Roman emperor Valerian. At one point in the grilling, Lawrence called out to his tormenters, "Turn me over. I'm done on this side."

The most compulsive case of diehard professionalism may be the pronouncement of the French grammarian Dominique Bouhours. As he departed this world at the age of 74, he uttered this model of linguistic propriety: "I am about to — or I am going to — die. Either is correct."

But the exit lines that we utter from our deathbed are not necessarily our last words to the world. Our curtain call and final message can be the epitaph (from a Greek word that means "tomb") inscribed on our gravestone. Epitaphs date back to the earliest Egyptians, but it was not until Elizabethan England that tombstone messages began to acquire literary and witty qualities.

Not all epitaphs are gravely serious. I am pleased to unveil some of the English-speaking world's funniest epitaphs, starting with epitaphs that demonstrate how some folk take their jobs with them to the grave.

Epitaph for a dentist:
Stranger: Approach this spot with gravity.
John Brown is filling his last cavity.

Epitaph for a lawyer:
Goembel, John E.
The defense rests.

Epitaph for an auctioneer:
Born 1828
Going!
Going!!
Gone!!!
1876

My favorite of these crypt-ic statements is an epitaph for a waiter:
By and by,
God caught his eye.

Some epitaphs show that punning can be a grave experience:

Epitaph for a drunkard:
He had his beer
From year to year,
And then his bier had him.

Epitaph for a golfer:
Guess What?
I'm six under.

About a woman who died from consumption:
It wasn't a cough that carried her off.
It was a coffin they carried her off in.

In a Georgetown burial ground:
I finally found a place to park!

In an English burial ground:
Here under the sod and under the trees
Is buried the body of Solomon Pease.
But in this hole lies only his pod.
His soul is shelled out and gone to God.

In an Irish burial ground:
Here lies Bridget O'Callaghan
Postmistress and Spinster
Returned — Unopened

Epitaph for an atheist:
All dressed up and no place to go.

Epitaph for a Wild West gunslinger:
Here lies Lester Moore.
Four slugs from a forty-four.
No Les. No More.

Some show business stars display a wisecrack on their not-so-grave stones.

Comedian Rodney Dangerfield:
There goes the neighborhood.

TV talk show host Merv Griffin:
I will not be back after this message.

Mel Blanc, the voice of Bugs Bunny:
That's all, folks!

ABRAHAM LINCOLN:
AMERICAN HUMORIST

Abraham Lincoln loved to infuse his statements with jokes that took on elements of parables. Of our sixteenth president a contemporary wrote, "When Lincoln tells a joke in a fireside group, his face loses its melancholy mask, his eyes sparkle, and his whole countenance lights up. And when he reaches the point in his narrative which invariably evokes the laughter of the crowd, nobody's enjoyment is greater than his."

Lincoln referred to laughter as "the joyful, beautiful, universal evergreen of life." In fact, he was our first presidential humorist. During the Civil War, London's *Saturday Review* told its readers, "One advantage the Americans have is the possession of a president who is not only the First Magistrate, but the Chief Joker of the Land."

The common people looked at him as one of their own. When he was running for the Illinois state legislature, an opponent of considerable standing dwelt on the fact that his father had been a senator, his grandfather a general and his uncle a congressman. Abe then rose to give his family background. "Ladies and gentlemen, I come from a long line of married folks. I don't know who my grandfather was. I am much more concerned to know what his grandson will be."

Abe Lincoln could make fun of himself, especially his gangly height and legendary homeliness. At six feet four inches, he was our loftiest American president. To the inevitable question

"How tall are you?" Lincoln would reply, "Tall enough to reach the ground."

The New York Herald described the president thusly: "Lincoln is the leanest, lankiest, most ungainly mass of legs, arms, and hatchet-face ever strung upon a single frame. He has most unwarrantably abused the privilege which all politicians have of being ugly."

During one of the Lincoln-Douglas debates, Stephen Douglas accused Lincoln of being two-faced. Replied Lincoln calmly, "I leave it to my audience: If I had two faces, would I be wearing this one?" When a grouchy old Democrat said to him, "They say you are a self-made man," Lincoln riposted, "Well, all I've got to say is that it was a damned bad job."

Early in the Civil War, committee of abolition war managers demanded that Ulysses S. Grant be removed from duty, charging that the general was a whiskey drinker and little better than a common drunkard.

Lincoln rejoined, "Well, I wish some of you would tell me the brand of whiskey that Grant drinks. I would like to send a barrel of it to my other generals."

During the Confederate attack on Fort Stevens in July 1864, Abraham Lincoln journeyed to the front to inspect Union defenses. The task of showing him around fell to young Oliver Wendell Holmes, Jr., aide to the commanding general, and a future Supreme Court Justice. When Holmes pointed out the enemy in the distance, Lincoln stood up—all six feet four of him with a stovepipe hat on top — to have a look.

A volley of musket fire spat from the enemy trenches. Grabbing the president by the arm, Holmes dragged him under cover and shouted, "Get down, you fool!" Realizing what he had said and to whom, Holmes was sure that disciplinary action would follow. To his immense relief, Lincoln rejoined, "Captain Holmes, I'm glad to see you know how to talk to a civilian."

When the Civil War ended on April 13, 1865, Lincoln gave orders to stop the draft of soldiers. The following day he made his fatal visit to Ford's Theatre to see *Our American Cousin*. At one point in the play, the heroine, reclining on a garden seat, calls for a shawl to protect her from the draft. The actor Edward Southern, to whom the request was addressed, replied on this occasion with this impromptu line: "You are mistaken, Miss Mary. The draft has already been stopped by order of the president!" Lincoln joined in the audience's appreciation of this timely quip with what was to be his last laughter.

My Famous Students

Teachers change lives, one lesson at a time. Almost everybody who is anybody was taught to be somebody by a teacher. I was an English teacher (an inmate in the House of Correction) for three decades, and I'm button-burstingly proud to share with you report card statements I wrote about students of mine who became famous:

In tense social situations, Marie Antoinette tends to lose her head. I recommend that she stop eating cake and go on a sugar-free diet.

Having Tommy Edison in my class has been an illuminating experience. He is very bright, and when he gets an idea, a light bulb seems to go on above his head.

Ludwig Van Beethoven behaves eccentrically in class. He hears music in his head even when he is not using an iPod. More seriously, all instructions from his teachers seem to fall on deaf ears.

Jefferson Davis prefers to play with just a small number of his classmates and doesn't join in activities designed for the entire group. His fellow students have voted him Most Likely to Secede.

Michelangelo is continually finger-painting on the ceiling, and the custodial staff has incurred considerable expense to scrub away his drawings.

Pablo Picasso exhibits possible talent in art, but he fails to show respect for authority. For example, despite my instructions, he continues to draw both eyes on the same side of each face.

Willie Shakespeare is failing Essay Writing because he refuses to write in prose, and his verse draws a blank with his classmates. In addition, he's always making a scene. If he continues in this manner, he will be Bard from the class.

Ptolemy needs to learn that the universe doesn't revolve around him.

Al Einstein is a problem child. He finds science and mathematics relatively easy, but he needs to pay more attention to his grooming.

Do you have any suggestions about how we can break Ivan Pavlov of his annoying habit of drooling every time the school bell rings?

Rodney Dangerfield wants to be the class clown, but his classmates give him no respect.

Because of his bullying and other forms of anti-social behavior, I have had to place Al Capone in a very long detention period.

Tiger Woods is doing very well in golf class but failing Driver's Education. While he drives well on a fairway, he doesn't fare well on a driveway.

Although Bernie Madoff is creative with figures, he is getting a D in Mathematics because his numbers just don't add up. Nonetheless, I am pleased to report that Bernie has been elected class treasurer.

As prom queen and captain of the cheerleading team, Sarah Palin is the most popular girl in the class. She is an aggressive debater, and her teammates have elected her vice president. But she struggles in Geography class, especially regarding the locations of Alaska and Russia.

Harry Houdini keeps his fellow students entertained with his amazing magic tricks. But his attendance record is dismal because he keeps disappearing.

I also taught fantastic students who exist only in my imagination:

Mary may have to be suspended. She is quite contrary and keeps bringing that darned lamb to school.

Georgie Porgie must stop kissing the girls and making them cry. I would like to see him play more with the boys, but Georgie just runs away from them.

The Big Bad Wolf is exhibiting anti-social tendencies. He has already blown two houses down and devoured at least one grandmother.

Jack shows great nimbleness and quickness in Physical Education. He is especially good at jumping over candlesticks, although he did happen to burn his butt and break his crown.

Humpty Dumpty had a great fall, but his grades and deportment deteriorated in the winter and spring. His boredom in the classroom has him climbing the walls, and his behavior has us all walking on eggshells. I think that he may suffer from restless egg syndrome.

Pinocchio exhibits a lot of passive-aggressive behavior. Sometimes he is everybody's puppet. At other times, he sticks his big nose in everybody's business.

Frosty the Snowman is a jolly, happy soul, but, in the cafeteria line, he loads up his plate with carrots so that he can pick his nose.

I wish Atlas would show more joy at school. He acts like he has the weight of the world on his shoulders.

I am impressed that the Cyclops has found the en-cyclops-pedia to be a real eye opener, but he just doesn't see eye to eyes with his classmates. In fact, he causes me a lot of trouble for only one pupil.

Narcissus appears to be too caught up in his own image. Yesterday he spent an hour staring at his reflection in the water in the boys' room toilet.

Sisyphus loves rock and roll, but that's all he does. He needs to find other outlets for his energy.

Pandora's box lunch is causing a lot of evil in the cafeteria.

Cain does not play well with others and has turned out to be a discipline problem. I have been willing to overlook some of his aggressive tendencies, but murdering one quarter of the earth's population goes beyond what I am able to tolerate.

Joshua is doing well in the horn section of the school orchestra, but I can no longer tolerate his blowing down the walls.

After numerous requests, Samson finally got his hair cut, but he has been failing Physical Education ever since. Perhaps he should be treated for fallen arches.

Moses has broken every commandment, but he demonstrates great ability with computers. He excels at downloading data from the cloud to his tablet.

David is a talented singer and player of stringed instruments, but he has broken dozens of school windows with his slingshot.

The Hulk is a star heavyweight on the school wrestling team, but his classmates tease him for his tattered clothing and green complexion. He does not react constructively to such criticism. I recommend that he attend an anger-management class.

Frankie Stein's antics in class keep us all in stitches, and many of his fellow students carry a torch for him. But I am deeply concerned that he may have a screw loose.

Dracula can be a real pain in the neck and can get under our skin. At times, he acts like a spoiled bat and drives us batty. But the young count is a dedicated student. He stays up all night studying for his blood tests, and in Mathematics, his blood count is the highest. I predict that he will graduate Phi Batta Cape-a.

The Mummy needs to learn to be more aware of the feelings of other pupils in the class. For now, she is too wrapped up in herself.

The Invisible Boy often lies to avoid punishment, but I can see right through him and find his fabrications to be quite transparent.

Darth Vader is constantly upsetting his classmates and tends to look on the dark side of things. His habitual smoking in the boys' room is starting to affect his breathing and his voice.

Being tall, dark, and hairy, King Kong thinks he has the girls in the palm of his hand. I wish he would break his habit of climbing up the school building and trying to catch a plane.

Robinson Crusoe is to be commended for his dedication to completing his assignments. He always gets his homework done by Friday.

I am at a loss to understand Henry Jekyll's mood swings. He demonstrates excellent deportment one day and horrible behavior the next.

Hester Prynne is a *straight-A* student, but her classmates have pilloried her for her accomplishments.

Sherlock Holmes earns high grades in all subjects requiring deductive reasoning. In fact, he tends to find school elementary.

Super Duper Bloopers

MINERS REFUSE TO WORK AFTER DEATH

American History
According to Student Bloopers

O ne of the fringe benefits of being an English or history teacher is receiving the occasional jewel of a student blooper in an essay or test paper. The original classroom blunder probably dates back to the day that some unsuspecting pupil first touched stylus to clay tablet. Ever since, students have demonstrated a remarkable facility for mixing up words that possess similar sounds but entirely different meanings or for goofing up the simplest of facts.

The results range from the pathetic to the hilarious to the unintentionally insightful. Sometimes the humor issues from a confusion between two words. Working independently, students have written, "Adolescence is that stage of life between puberty and adultery," "Having one wife is called monotony," "When a man has more than one wife, he is a pigamist," "A man who marries twice commits bigotry," and "Acrimony is what a man gives his divorced wife." And, substituting a *q* for a *g*, a young scholar once wrote, "When a boy and a girl are deeply in love, there is no quilt felt between them."

Sidesplitting slips like these are collected by teachers throughout the world who don't mind sharing a little humor while taking their jobs seriously. For example, William Lyon Phelps of Yale University found this sentence gleaming out of a student essay: "The girl tumbled down the stairs and lay prostitute at the bottom." In the margin of the paper, the professor commented, "My dear sir, you must learn to distinguish between a fallen woman and one who has merely slipped."

Even better, methinks, is this report from Carl Cochran, a private school English teacher. Early in the school year, Mr. Cochran assigned an essay asking students to write about what they did during the previous summer. One student wrote about having worked in Venezuela for an oil company, but continually waxed enthusiastic about the "burrows" that he rode. The teacher wrote this comment at the end of the essay: "My dear young man: This a fine essay, but you really must learn the difference between a burro and a burrow. Otherwise, people will think that you don't know the difference between your ass and a hole in the ground."

It is truly astounding what havoc students can wreak upon the chronicles of the human race. I have pasted together the following "history" of the world from genuine, certified, authentic student bloopers collected by teachers, from eighth grade through college level. These gems are worthy of a Pullet Surprise (yet another student blooper).

Read carefully, and you will learn a lot.

The inhabitants of ancient Egypt buried their mummies and daddies in the pyramids, and they all wrote in hydraulics. They lived in the Sarah Dessert, over which they traveled by Camelot. The climate of the Sarah is such that the inhabitants have to live elsewhere, so certain areas of the dessert are cultivated by irritation. Ancient Egyptian women wore a *kalasiris,* a loose-fitting garment which started just below the breasts which hung to the floor.

The Bible is full of interesting caricatures. In the first book of the Bible, Guinness, God got tired of creating the world, so he took the sabbath off. Adam and Eve were created from an apple tree. One of their children, Cain, once asked, "Am I my brother's son?" Noah's wife was called Joan of Ark. He built an ark, and the animals came onboard in pears.

Lot's wife was a pillar of salt by day and a ball of fire by night. Sampson was a strongman who let himself be led astray by a jezebel like Delilah.

God asked Abraham to sacrifice Isaac on Mount Montezuma. Jacob, son of Isaac, stole his brother's birthmark. Jacob was a patriarch who brought up his 12 sons to be patriarchs, but they did not take to it. One of Jacob's sons, Joseph, gave refuse to the Israelites.

Pharaoh forced the Hebrew slaves to make bread without straw. Moses led them to the Red Sea, where they made unleavened bread, which is bread without any ingredients. The Egyptians all drowned in the dessert. Afterward, Moses went up on Mount Cyanide to get the Ten Commandments, but he died before he ever reached Canada.

Joshua fought the Battle of Geritol. David was a Hebrew king skilled at playing the liar. He fought the Finkelsteins, a race of people who lived in biblical times, Solomon, one of David's sons, had 300 wives and 700 porcupines.

Jesus was born because Mary had an immaculate contraption. When May heard that she was the mother of Jesus, she sang the Magna Carta. When the three wise guys from the east side arrived, they found Jesus in the manager. When he grew up, Jesus enunciated the Golden Rule, which says to do unto other before they do one to you.

The Greeks were a highly sculptured people, and without them, we wouldn't have history. The Greeks invented three kinds of columns — Corinthian, Ironic, and Dork. They also created myths. A myth is a female moth. One myth says that the mother of Achilles dipped him in the river Stynx until he became intolerable.

Achilles appears in the *Iliad*, by Homer. Homer also wrote the *Oddity*, in which Penelope was the last hardship that Ulysses endured on his journey. Socrates was a famous Greek teacher who went around giving people advice. They killed him. Socrates died from an overdose of wedlock.

In the Olympic Games, Greeks ran races, jumped, hurled the biscuits, and threw the Java. The reward to the victor was a coral wreath. The government of Athens was democratic because people took the law into their own hands.

Eventually, the Romans came along and conquered the Geeks. History calls people Romans because they never stayed in one place for very long. At Roman banquets, the guests wore garlics in their hair. Julius Caesar extinguished himself on the battlefields of Gaul. The Ides of March murdered him because they thought he was going to be made king. Caesar expired with these immortal words upon his dying lips: "Eat you, Brutus!" Nero was a cruel tyranny who would torture his poor subjects by playing the fiddle to them.

The Romans were overrun by the ball bearings. Then came the Middle Ages, when everyone was middle aged. King Alfred conquered the Dames. He lived in the age of shivery, with brave knights on prancing horses and beautiful women. King Harold mustarded his troops before the Battle of Hastings. Joan of Arc was burnt to a steak and canonized by Bernard Shaw. People contracted the blue bonnet plague, which caused them to grow boobs on their necks.

Magna Carta provided that no free man should be hanged twice for the same offense. People performed morality plays, about ghosts, goblins, virgins, and other mythical creatures.

In mid evil times, most of the people were alliterate. The greatest writer of the time was Chaucer, who wrote many poems and verses and also wrote literature. Another tale tells of William Tell, who shot an arrow through an apple while standing on his son's head.

The Renaissance was an age in which more individuals felt the value of their human being. Martin Luther was nailed to the church door at Wittenberg for selling papal indulgences. He died a horrible death, being excommunicated by a bull.

The Renaissance was an age of great inventions and discoveries. Gutenberg invented the Bible and removable type. Sir Walter Raleigh discovered cigarettes and started smoking. And Sir Francis Drake circumcised the world with a 100-foot clipper.

The greatest writer of the Renaissance was William Shakespeare. Shakespeare never made much money and is famous only because of his plays. He lived at Windsor with his merry wives, writing tragedies, comedies, and errors. In one of Shakespeare's plays, Hamlet rations out his situation by relieving himself in a long soliloquy. In another, Lady Macbeth tries to convince Macbeth to kill the king by attacking his manhood. Romeo and Juliet are an example of a heroic couplet. In *Julius Caesar,* the toothslayer warned Caesar to beware the March of Dimes.

Writing at the same time as Shakespeare was Miguel Cervantes. He wrote *Donkey Hote.* The next great author was John Milton. Milton wrote *Paradise Lost.* Then his wife died, and he wrote *Paradise Regained.*

During the Renaissance America began. Christopher Columbus was a great navigator who discovered America while cursing about the Atlantic on the Nina, the Pintacolada, and the Santa Fe.

One of the causes of the Revolutionary War was the English put tacks on their tea. Also, the colonists would send their parcels through the post without stamps. Finally, the colonists won the war and no longer had to pay for taxis.

The United States was founded by four fathers. Delegates from the original 13 states formed the Contented Congress. Thomas Jefferson, a Virgin, and Benjamin Franklin were two singers of the Declaration of Independence. Franklin had gone to Boston carrying all his clothes in his pocket and a loaf of bread under each arm. He invented electricity by rubbing cats backwards and declared, "A horse divided against itself cannot stand." Franklin died in 1790 and is still dead.

George Washington married Martha Curtis and in due time became the Father of Our Country. Then the Constitution of the United States was adopted to secure domestic hostility. Under the Constitution, the people enjoyed the right to keep bare arms.

Abraham Lincoln became America's greatest precedent. Lincoln's mother died in infancy, and he was born in a log cabin which he built with his very own hands. When Lincoln was president, he wore only a tall silk hat. He said, "In onion there is strength." President Lincoln wrote the Gettysburg Address while traveling from Washington to Gettysburg on the back of an envelope.

On the night of April 14, 1865, Lincoln went to the theater and got shot in his seat by one of the actors in the moving picture show. The believed assinator was John Wilkes Booth, a supposingly insane actor. This ruined Booth's career.

Meanwhile in Europe, the Enlightenment was a reasonable time. Voltaire invented electricity. Gravity was invented by Isaac Walton. It is chiefly noticeable in the autumn, when the apples are falling off the trees.

Johann Sebastian Bach wrote a lot of music and had a great many children. He kept an old spinster up in his attic on which he practiced every day. Bach died from 1750 to the present. Bach was the most famous composer in the world, and so was Handel. Handel was half-German, half-Italian, and half-English. Ludwig van Beethoven wrote music even though he was deaf. He was so deaf he wrote loud music. He took long walks in the forest even when everyone was calling for him. Beethoven expired in 1827 and later died for this.

France was in a very serious state. The French Revolution was accomplished before it happened. The Marseillaise was the theme song of the French Revolution, and it catapulted into Napoleon. During the Napoleonic Wars, the crowned heads of Europe were trembling in their shoes. Then the Spanish gorillas came down from the hills and nipped at Napoleon's flanks. He wanted an heir to inherit his power, but since Josephine was a baroness, she couldn't bear children.

The sun never set on the British Empire because the British Empire is in the east and the sun sets in the west. Queen Victoria was the longest queen. She sat on a thorn for 63 years. Her reclining years were exemplatory of a great personality. Her death was the final event which ended her reign.

The nineteenth century was a time of many great inventions and thoughts. The invention of the steamboat caused a network of rivers to spring up. Samuel Morse invented a code of telepathy. Louis Pasteur discovered a cure for rabbis. Charles Darwin was a naturalist who wrote the *Organ of the Species,* Madman Curie discovered radio, and Karl Marx became one of the Marx Brothers.

The First World War was caused by the assignation of the Arch-Duck by an anahist. Wilt Chamberlain practiced appeasement in Europe before the Second World War thinking that it would stop

Hitler and the Nazis. In the Second World War Franklin Roosevelt put a stop to Hitler, who committed suicide in his bunk.

Martin Luther had a dream. He went to Washington and recited his Sermon on the Monument. Later, he nailed 96 Protestants in the Watergate Scandal, which ushered in a new error in the anals of human history.

HEADLINE HOWLERS

The English language and the game of baseball would be immeasurably poorer without the fractured diction and unruly grammar of St. Louis Cardinals pitcher and broadcaster Dizzy Dean. Dean peppered his commentary with *ain'ts*, double negatives, and colorful verbs, such as "He slud into third base" and "The pitcher flang the ball."

When an indignant listener complained, "Mr. Dean, don't you know the King's English?" Dizzy reflected for a moment and replied, "Sure I do — and so's the Queen!"

While pitching in the 1934 World Series, Dean tried to break up a double play and was struck in the head by the relay throw. The force of the baseball knocked him unconscious and sent the daffy pitcher to the hospital.

Luckily, Dean was not seriously injured, and the next day a headline blared:

X-RAYS OF DEAN'S HEAD REVEAL NOTHING

One of comedian Will Rogers' favorite remarks was "All I know is what I read in the papers." For many busy people, all they know is what they read in the headlines. The bold messages entice readers to dive more deeply into a story.

Behind every newspaper headline lurks a newspaper deadline. The men and women who compose headlines work within pressing restrictions. They must pack large-size print into narrow column widths, and their compact messages must clearly state the theme of each story, keep words intact, be attractive to the eye, and catch the reader's attention. On top of that, each headline must be written quickly. No wonder that, on occasion, editors get caught with their headlines down, and, exposed to as many as several million readers, the bold-face botch becomes a red-face result.

Some of the best two-headed headlines are those in which an inadvertent pun lifts the message from the blandly literal to the sublimely absurd:

GRANDMOTHER OF EIGHT
MAKES HOLE IN ONE

KIDS MAKE NUTRITIOUS SNACKS

DEFENDANT'S SPEECH ENDS IN LONG SENTENCE

FRIED CHICKEN IN MICROWAVE
WINS TRIP TO HAWAII

MAN STRUCK BY LIGHTNING
FACES BATTERY CHARGE

ASBESTOS SUIT PRESSED

FLAMING TOILET SEAT CAUSES
EVACUATION AT HIGH SCHOOL

HOUSE PASSES GAS
TAX ONTO SENATE

TUNA BITING OFF WASHINGTON COAST

ALLIES PUSH BOTTLES UP 10,000 GERMANS
TRAFFIC DEAD RISE SLOWLY

U'S FOOD SERVICE
FEEDS THOUSANDS,
GROSSES MILLIONS

COUNTY OFFICIALS TO TALK RUBBISH

THUGS EAT THEN ROB PROPRIETOR

ROBBER HOLDS UP ALBERT'S HOSIERY

FARMER BILL DIES IN HOUSE

IRAQI HEAD SEEKS ARMS

When a newspaper goes out wearing the wrong banners, its messages can become unwittingly suggestive:

QUEEN MARY HAVING BOTTOM SCRAPED

IS THERE A RING OF DEBRIS AROUND URANUS?

HENSHAW OFFERS
RARE OPPORTUNITY
TO GOOSE HUNTERS

HIGH COURT TO HEAR MARIJUANA CASE

STUD TIRES OUT

PROSTITUTES APPEAL TO POPE

GROVER MAN DRAWS PRISON TERM,
FINE FOR SEX ACTS

PANDA MATING FAILS;

VETERINARIAN TAKES OVER

IDAHO GROUP ORGANIZES
TO HELP SERVICE WIDOWS

COLUMNIST GETS UROLOGIST
IN TROUBLE WITH HIS PEERS

DR. RUTH TO TALK ABOUT SEX
WITH NEWSPAPER EDITORS

STERILIZATION SOLVES PROBLEMS FOR PETS, OWNERS

ORGAN FESTIVAL ENDS IN SMASHING CLIMAX

Sometimes the galley gaffe issues from an ambiguity in grammar:

BRITISH LEFT WAFFLES ON FALKLAND ISLANDS

EYE DROPS OFF SHELF

TEACHER STRIKES IDLE KIDS

SQUAD HELPS DOG BITE VICTIM

AMERICAN SHIPS HEAD TO LIBYA

MAN EATING PIRANHA
MISTAKENLY SOLD AS PET FISH

ENRAGED COW INJURES FARMER WITH AX

ADMITS SHOOTING HUSBAND
FROM STAND DURING TRIAL

YOUTH HIT BY CAR RIDING BICYCLE

STOLEN PAINTING FOUND BY TREE

BE SURE TO EAT RIGHT BEFORE SURGERY

SILENT TEAMSTER BOSS GETS
UNUSUAL PUNISHMENT, LAWYER

2 SISTERS REUNITED AFTER 18 YEARS
IN CHECKOUT LINE

Then come the headlines that have fallen under a spell

ESCAPEE CAPTURED
AFTER 10 DAYS ON THE LAMB

U.N. PEACEKEEPERS LAND
IN LIBERIA TO REIGN IN VIOLENCE

2 MEN ARRESTED FOR HEROINE TRAFFICKING

Occasionally, a deformed headline takes on a meaning that is exactly the opposite of the one intended:

NEVER WITHHOLD
HERPES INFECTION
FROM LOVED ONE

AUTOS KILLING 110 A DAY
LET'S RESOLVE TO DO BETTER

20-YEAR FRIENDSHIP ENDS AT ALTAR

And sometimes the headline illuminates the painfully obvious:

WAR DIMS HOPE FOR PEACE

IF STRIKE ISN'T SETTLED QUICKLY,
IT MAY LAST AWHILE

JAIL MAY HAVE TO CLOSE DOORS

COLD WAVE LINKED TO TEMPERATURES

BLIND WOMAN GETS NEW KIDNEY
FROM DAD SHE HASN'T SEEN IN YEARS

SENSE FOUL PLAY IN DEATH
OF MAN FOUND BOUND AND HANGED

ENFIELD COUPLE SLAIN;
POLICE SUSPECT HOMICIDE

SOMETHING WENT WRONG
IN JET CRASH, EXPERT SAYS

TYPHOON RIPS THROUGH CEMETERY
HUNDREDS DEAD

STUDY FINDS SEX, PREGNANCY LINK

UNAPPETIZING MENUS

- A Japanese restaurant cautions "Menus Are for Eating Customers Only."
- A Swiss restaurant boasts "Our Wines Leave You Nothing to Hope For."
- An Indian restaurant advertises "We Serve Tea in a Bag Like Mother."
- A Shanghai Mongolian hot-pot buffet guarantees "You Will Be Able to Eat All You Wish Until You are Fed Up."
- An establishment in Cairo assures patrons that "The Drinking Water in This Restaurant Has Been Passed by The Authorities."

Hungry? Here's a "full-coarse meal" I've put together consisting of skewed and skewered items spotted by tourists around the world. Bon appétit!

Soup
Cup $5 / Bowel $8

Gritty Balloons in Soup   Fisherman's Crap Soup

Barely Soup   Soap of the Day

Limpid Red Beet Soup

Cheesy Dumplings in the Form of a Finger

Salad
Salad, a Firm's Own Make   Groin Salad

Thai Style Uterus Salad

Meat

Buff Steak
Warm Little Dogs
Calf Pluck
Roast Beast
Sir Loin
Meat Dumping
Irritable Scalloped Kidney

Gut Casserole
Hambugger
Dreaded Veal Cutlets
Pork with Fresh Garbage
Liver Worst
Demonic Steak
Amiable and Sour Pork

Beef Rashers Beaten Up in the Country People's Fashion

Poultry

Chicken Low Mein
Hen Fried with Butler
Chicken in a Casket
Foul Breast

Frayed Chicken
Goose Barnacles
Chicken Pox Pie
Roasted Duck Let Loose

Utmost of Chicken Fried in Bother
Lightly Flowered Chicken Breast

Vegetables

Priest Fainted Eggplant

Muchrooms

Cabitch   Mushed Potatoes

Potato Cheeps

Sundries

Antipaste
Toes with Butter & Jam
Fried Hormones
Fried Swarm
Spaghetti Fungoole

Baked Zit
Mixed Boils to Pick
Muffled Frog Rumps
Gollum Shrimp
Drunken Prawns in Spit

Tortilla Topped with Melted Cheese,
Sour Cream, and Glaucoma

Desserts

Lady's Finger
Strawberry Crap
Chocolate Sand Kooky

Tart of the House
Chocolate Mouse Tort
Chocolate Puke

Beverages

White Whine   Turkey Coffee

Special Cocktail for Women with Nuts

Signs of the Times

Recently, my family enjoyed a delicious meal at one of our downtown restaurants. When we entered the establishment, we were greeted by a sign that read "Please Wait for Hostess to Be Seated." So we stood around for a while waiting for our hostess to sit down, but she never did.

Restaurants across our fair land display a riotous array of signs that are a bubble off plumb. My collection includes "Eat Here and Get Gas," "Customers Who Consider Our Waitresses Uncivil Ought to See the Manager," "Open Seven Days a Week and Weekends," "Help Keep the Birds Healthy. Don't Feed Them Restaurant Food," "Yes, We are Open. Sorry for the Inconvenience," and "Shoes are Required to Eat Inside."

Before I sign off, I share more signs that need to be re-signed, sign language that contains the kind of goofy prose that laughs in the face of logic:

At a gas station: We will sell gasoline to anyone in a glass container.

In a jewelry store: Ears pierced while you wait.

On an abbey: Trespassers will be prosecuted to the full extent of the law. -Sisters of Mercy

In a dry-cleaning store: Thirty-eight years on the same spot.

In another dry-cleaning store: We don't tear your clothing with machinery. We do it carefully by hand.

In a casino bathroom: Toilet Out of Order. Please Use Floor Below.

In a department store: Bargain Basement Upstairs.

In a dance hall: Good clean dancing every night but Sunday.

At a photography studio: Now shooting seniors for free.

In a maternity ward: No children allowed.

In a drugstore: We dispense with accuracy.

In the office of a loan company: Ask about our plans for owning your home.

In a convalescent home: For the sick and tired of the Episcopal Church

On the entrance to a repair shop: We can repair anything. Please knock hard on the door, as the doorbell is broken.

In another shop: Our motto is to give our customers the lowest possible prices and workmanship.

In a number of parking areas: Violators will be enforced and trespassers will be violated.

On a display of "I Love You Only" Valentine cards: Now available in multi-packs.

In the window of an appliance store: Don't kill your wife. Let our washing machines do the dirty work.

In a funeral parlor: Ask about our layaway plan.

In a clothing store: Wonderful bargains for men with 16 and 17 necks.

In another clothing store: Men's wool suits. They won't last an hour!

On a shopping mall marquee: Archery tournament. Ears pierced.

Outside a country shop: We buy junk and sell antiques.

In the window of a general store: Why go elsewhere to be cheated, when you can come here?

In a conference center: Psychic fair cancelled due to unforeseen circumstances.

In a cemetery: Persons are prohibited from picking flowers from any but their own graves.

On a movie marquee: Now Playing: ADAM AND EVE with a cast of thousands!

In front of a car wash: If you can't read this, it's time you wash your car.

On garment bags: To avoid suffocation, keep away from children.

Outside a secondhand shop: We exchange anything — bicycles, washing machines, etc. Why not bring your wife along and get a wonderful bargain?

In a safari park: Elephants, please stay in your car.

Notice in a farmer's field: The farmer allows walkers to cross the field, but the bull charges.

In a laundromat: Automatic washing machines. Please remove all your clothes when the light goes out.

On a radiator repair garage: Best place to take a leak

One of my favorite categories of loopy sign language is listings that are stacked up into Towers of Babble:

On a farm:

FLOWERS

PRODUCE

EGGS

In the entrance to a camera store:

NO

DOGS

EATING

BICYCLES

On the front of a club:

LIVE LOBSTERS

DANCING NIGHTLY

In a department store:

WE HAVE BUTTON-FLY LEVIS

OPEN TILL 10 TONITE

At a farmers' market:

GIANT BLUEBERRIES

SQUASH

NATIVE CORN

On a movie theater marquee:

ERIN BROCKOVICH
SCREWED
MY DOG SKIP

DISORDER IN THE COURT

Hear ye! Hear ye!

Most language is spoken language, and most words, once they are uttered, vanish forever into thin air. But such is not the case with speech spoken during trials, for there exists an army of court reporters whose job it is to take down and preserve every statement made during the proceedings. I congratulate court reporters for keeping a straight face while recording these court jesters.

Court is now in session, and here are my favorite "transquips," all preserved by America's keepers of the word:

Q. What is your brother-in-law's name?
A. Borofkin.
Q. What is his first name?
A. I can't remember.
Q. He's been your brother-in-law for 45 years, and you can't remember his first name?
A. No. I tell you I'm too excited. [Rising from the witness chair and pointing to Mr. Borofkin] Nathan, for God's sake, tell them your first name!

Q. Did you stay all night with this man in New York?
A. I refuse to answer that question.
Q. Did you stay all night with this man in Chicago?
A. I refuse to answer that question.

49

Q. Did you ever stay all night with this man in Miami?
A. No.

Q. James stood back and shot Tommy Lee?
A. Yes.
Q. And then Tommy Lee pulled out his gun and shot James in the fracas?
A. No sir, just above it.

Q. Was the child born out of wedlock?
A. No, sir, just outside of Louisville.

Q. You say this woman shot her husband at close range with his pistol.
A. Yes, sir. That's right.
Q. Any powder marks on his body?
A. Yes, sir. That's why she shot him.

Q. How did you happen to go to Dr. Cheney?
A. Well, a gal down the road had had several of her children by Dr. Cheney and said he was really good.

Q. Did he pick the dog up by the ears?
A. No.

Q. What was he doing with the dog's ears?
A. Picking them up in the air.
Q. Where was the dog at this time?
A. Attached to the ears.

Q. Can you write?
A. Yes sir, I can write a little.
Q. Have you ever been in a penitentiary?
A. Yes, sir.
Q. What for?
A. Forgery.

Q. You say you're innocent, yet five people swore they saw you steal a watch.
A. Your Honor, I can produce 500 people who didn't see me steal it.

Q. What can you tell us about the truthfulness and veracity of this defendant?
A. she'll tell you the truth. She said she was going to kill the son of a gun — and she did.

Before we move on to another category, let's listen in on one last exchange involving Gary, a child:

Q. And lastly, Gary, all your responses must be oral, O.K?
A. Oral.

JUDGE. I know you, don't I?

DEFENDANT. Uh, yes, Your Honor.

JUDGE. All right, tell me, how do I know you?

DEFENDANT. Judge, do I have to tell you?

JUDGE. Of course, you might be obstructing justice not to tell me.

DEFENDANT. Okay, I was your bookie.

JUDGE. Well, sir. I have reviewed this case, and I've decided to give your wife $775 each week.

HUSBAND. That's fair, Your Honor. I'll try to send her a few bucks myself.

JUDGE. Well, gentlemen of the jury, are you unanimous?

FOREMAN. Yes, your Honor, we're all alike — temporarily insane.

JUDGE. Now, as we begin, I must ask you to banish all present information and prejudice from your minds, if you have any.

JUDGE. The charge here is theft of frozen chickens. Are you the defendant?

DEFENDANT. No, sir, I'm the guy who stole the chickens.

JUDGE. Is there any reason you could not serve as a juror in this case?

JUROR. I don't want to be away from my job that long.

JUDGE. Can't they do without you at work?

JUROR. Yes, but I don't want them to know it.

JUDGE. Please identify yourself for the record.

DEFENDANT. Colonel Ebenezer Jackson.

JUDGE. What does the "Colonel" stand for?

DEFENDANT. Well, it's kind of like the "Honorable" in front of your name—not a damn thing.

DEFENDANT (after being sentenced to 90 days in jail). Can I address the court?

JUDGE. Of course.

DEFENDANT. If I called you a son of a bitch, what would you do?

JUDGE. I'd hold you in contempt and assess an additional five days in jail.

DEFENDANT. What if I thought you were a son of a bitch?

JUDGE. I can't do anything about that. There's no law against thinking.

DEFENDANT. In that case, I think you're a son of a bitch.

Sometimes a jurist gets a chance to strike back with their gavel. A defendant pleaded, "Your Honor. As God is my judge, I didn't do it. I'm not guilty."

Replied the judge, "He isn't! I am! You did! You are!"

Before we recess, I offer a slate of stupid lawyer questions. Remember it takes years of law school and more years of courtroom experience to cross-examine like this:

Q. Doctor, how many autopsies have you performed on dead people?
A. All my autopsies have been on dead people.

Q. Do you recall approximately the time that you examined the body of Mr. Dunnington at the Rose Chapel?
A. The autopsy started about 8:30 pm.
Q. And Mr. Dunnington was dead at the time. Is that correct?
A. No, you dumbass. He was sitting there on the table wondering why I was doing an autopsy!

Q. Were you acquainted with the decedent?
A. Yes, sir.
Q. Before or after he died?

Q. Do you know how far pregnant you are right now?
A. I will be three months November 8th.
Q. Apparently then, the date of conception was August 8th?
A. Yes.
Q. What were you and your husband doing at that time?

Q. What happened then?

A. He told me, he says, "I have to kill you because you can identify me."

Q. Did he kill you?

A. No.

Q. I understand you're Bernie Davis's mother.

A. Yes.

Q. How long have you known him?

Q. Now I'm going to show you what has been marked as State's
Exhibit No. 2 and ask if you recognize the picture.

A. That's me.

Q. Were you present when that picture was taken?

Court is adjourned!

ELECTILE DYSFUNCTION

Ambrose Bierce sardonically defined politics as "a strife of interests masquerading as a contest of principles," and Peter DeVries defined a politician as "a man who can be verbose in fewer words than anyone else." Many mean things have been said about politicians. They have even been skewered by a fanciful etymology for the word *politics: Poly,* as in *polygon, polyglot, polygamy,* and *polytheistic,* means "many" — and *tics,* well, tics are blood-sucking parasites!

Politicians have been riddled by riddles:

Why are there so many political jokes? Because we keep electing them.

What is a politician? A man who will double-cross a bridge when he comes to it.

How can you tell when a politician is lying? His lips are moving.

How are politicians like diapers? They both need frequent changing — and for the same reason.

What's the difference between a centaur and a senator? One is half man and half horse's ass — and the other is a creature in mythology.

Many a poli-tickle has disgorged from the golden throats and silver tongues of our appointed and anointed representatives in government. Let's start with some of our presidents:

When a great many people are unable to find work, unemployment results. -*Calvin Coolidge*

If Lincoln were alive today, he'd roll over in his grave. -*Gerald Ford*

I believe that this country's policies should be heavily biased in favor of nondiscrimination. -*Bill Clinton*

We have here two incredibly credible witnesses. -*Joe Biden,* who once exclaimed, "That's the most unheard-of thing I ever heard of!"

Nonpareil pearls of wisdom from our mayors::

I have reiterated over and over again what I have said before. -*New York mayor Robert Wagner*

Outside of the killings, Washington has one of the lowest crime rates in the country -*D.C. mayor Marion Barry*

The streets in Philadelphia are safe. It's only the people who make them unsafe. -*Philadelphia mayor Frank Rizzo*

The police are not here to create disorder. They are here to preserve disorder. -*Chicago mayor Richard Daley*

Political tickles from our governors:

The bankers' pockets are bulging with the sweat of the honest working man. -*New Hampshire governor John Sununu*

My vision is to make California the most diverse state on earth, and we have people from every planet on the earth in this state. -*California governor Gray Davis*

I think that gay marriages are something that should be between a man and a woman. -*California governor Arnold Schwarzenegger*

This is the worst disaster in California since I've been elected. -*California governor Pat Brown, reacting to a flood*

I didn't say that I didn't say it. I said that I didn't say that I said it. I want to make that perfectly clear. -*Michigan governor George Romney*

Let's close with some thud and blunder from the mouths of other officials.

There are known knowns. These are things that we know we know. There are known unknowns. That is to say, there are things that we know we don't know. But there are also unknown unknowns. There are things we don't know we don't know. -*Secretary of Defense Donald Rumsfeld*

Capital punishment is our society's recognition of the sanctity of human life. *-Utah senator Orrin Hatch*

If English was good enough for Jesus Christ, then it's good enough for me *-attributed to Georgia congresswoman Marjorie Taylor Green and others*

It's a Punderful Life!

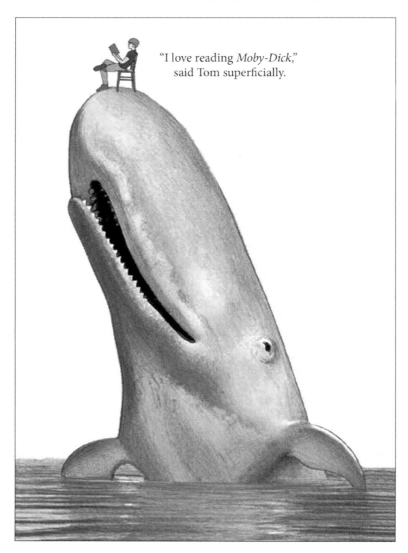

"I love reading *Moby-Dick*," said Tom superficially.

Jest for the Pun of it

In America, we celebrate just about everything, so it may come as no surprise to you that early each January, pun-up girls and pun gents observe National Save the Pun Week. I've been a punographer all my life and truly believe that the pun is worth celebrating all year round. After all, the pun is mightier than the sword, and these days you are much more likely to run into a pun than into a sword.

Scoffing at puns is a conditioned reflex, and through the centuries, groan-ups have aimed a steady barrage of libel and slander at the practice of punning. More than three centuries ago, the playwright and critic John Dennis sneered, "A pun is the lowest form of wit," a charge that has been butted and rebutted by a mighty line of pundits and punheads.

Author Henry Erskine, for example, protested that if a pun is the lowest form of wit, "it is therefore the foundation of all wit." Versatile entertainer Oscar Levant added a tagline: "A pun is the lowest form of humor — when you don't think of it first." International Save the Pun Foundation president John Crosbie bakes this hot, cross pun: "If someone complains that punning is the lowest form of humor, you can tell them that poetry is verse." Having been elected International Punster of the Year, I proclaim, "A bun is indeed the doughiest form of wheat — earthy humus that everybody digs."

Lexicographer Samuel Johnson, the self-appointed custodian of the English language, once thundered, "To trifle with the vocabulary which is the vehicle of social intercourse is to tamper with the currency of human intelligence. He who would violate the sanctities of the Mother Tongue would invade the recesses of the national till without remorse." If language is money and language manipulators are thieves, Doctor Johnson was a felon, for to him is attributed the following:

> I should be punishéd
> For every pun I shed.
> Do not leave a puny shred
> Of my punnish head!

This little ditty proves the truth of essayist Joseph Addison's pronouncement "The Seeds of Punning are in the Minds of all Men, and tho' they may be subdued by Reason, Reflection, and Good Sense they will be very apt to shoot up in the greatest Genius that is not broken and cultivated by the Rules of Art."

No one is sure of the origin of the word *pun,* but the best guess is that *pun* is a shortening of the Italian *puntiglio,* "a small or fine point." Punning is a rewording experience. The inveterate punster believes that a good pun is like a good steak — a rare medium well done. In such a prey on words, *rare, medium,* and *well done* are double entendres, so that six meanings are crammed into the space ordinarily occupied by just three.

Punnery is largely the trick of compacting two or more ideas within a single word or expression. Punnery surprises us by flouting the law of nature that pretends that two things cannot occupy the same space at the same time. It is an exercise of the mind in being concise.

That many people groan rather than laugh at puns doesn't mean that the punnery isn't funnery. If the pun is a good one, the groan usually signifies a kind of suppressed admiration for the verbal acrobatics on display, and perhaps a hidden envy. Edgar Allan Poe (of all people) pointed out that "of puns it has been said that those most dislike who are least able to utter them."

Pun for all and all for pun! I entered ten puns in a humor contest hoping that one would win—but no pun in ten did. Nonetheless, using the criteria of verbal pyrotechnics, humor, and enduring pop-ularity of the play on words, I present my picks for the top dozen blue-ribbin' puns of all time. Sharpen your pun cells, O pun pals. Let's get to wit:

12. Did you hear about the math teacher who went on a diet? First, she gave up pi — and when that didn't work, she decided to trinomials.

11. A priest, a minister, and a rabbit walk into a blood bank to donate blood. A nurse asks each of them to provide their blood type. Says the rabbit, "I'm pretty sure I'm a Type O."

10. What do you get when you cross a gorilla with a clay worker? A Hairy Potter!

9. What do you get when you cross an elephant with a rhinoc-eros? Elephino!

8. Outside of a dog, a book is a man's best friend. Inside of a dog, it's too dark to read. -*Groucho Marx*

7. Satan has started a wig manufacturing business. It's called Devil Make Hair, and its most popular product is the Hell Toupee.

6. Two ropes walk into a Wild West saloon. The first rope goes up to the bar and orders a beer. "We don't serve ropes in this saloon," sneers the bartender, and he picks up the rope, whirls him around in the air, and tosses him out into the street.

"Oh, oh. I'd better disguise myself," thinks the second rope. He ruffles up his ends to make himself look rougher and twists himself into a circle to look bigger. Then he too sidles up to the bar.

"Hmmm. Are you one of them ropes?" snarls the bartender.

"I'm a frayed knot."

5. A man gave his male offspring a cattle ranch and named it focus — because it was a place where the sun's rays meet and the sons raise meat.

4. Marriage is like a deck of cards. You start off with two hearts and a diamond — and pretty soon, you want to grab a club and use a spade.

3. One of the greatest men of the twentieth century was the political leader and ascetic Mahatma Gandhi. His denial of the

earthly pleasures included the fact that he never wore anything on his feet and walked barefoot everywhere. Moreover, he ate so little that he developed delicate health and very bad breath. Thus, he became known as a super-callused fragile mystic hexed by halitosis!

2. You'd better watch out, or my karma will run over your dogma.

And my numero-uno pun of all time, created by the incomparable Dorothy Parker: I'd rather have a bottle in front of me than a frontal lobotomy!

Best Bar Jokes—Bar None

Charles Dickens walks into a bar and orders a martini. The bartender asks, "Olive or twist?"

Rene Descartes walks into a bar, and the bartender asks him if he'd like a drink. Descartes replies, "I think not" — and POOF, he disappears.

A horse walks into a bar, and the bartender asks, "Why the long face?"

The horse says, "I'm depressed."

The bartender wonders, "Maybe that's because you drink too much. Might you be an alcoholic?"

The horse says, "I don't think I am" — and POOF, *he* disappears.

(Did you notice that in the last two jokes I put Descartes before the horse?)

The formula "A(n) _____ walks into a bar" has provided the take-off point for scads of jokes over the years. Here's an in-bar scenario that centers on grammar and rhetoric:

An oxymoron walks into a bar. The silence is deafening as she orders some fresh-frozen jumbo shrimp.

Then, taking everything for granite, a malapropism walks into the same bar, looking for all intensive purposes like a wolf in cheap clothing, muttering epitaphs and casting dispersions.

A mixed metaphor then walks into the bar. She has a mind like a steel sieve and kindles a flood of attention from the crowd.

A paradox walk into the bar; they examine everybody.

A cliché walks into the bar, looking busy as a beaver and a bee, happy as a clam, a lark, and a pig in spit, and crazy as a bedbug, a coot, and a loon. Everybody in the bar avoids the cliché like the plague.

Then into the bar walks a misplaced modifier with a glass eye named Hilda.

A missing Oxford comma turns up at the bar. He spends the evening watching the television getting drunk and smoking cigars.

A furious palindrome stomps into the bar. "Yo, boy!" she shouts, "Dammit! I'm mad!" The crowd enthuses, "Wow!," "Yay!," "Hey, yeh!," and "Ah ha!" A few ask, "Huh?"

Faster than greased lightning, a hyperbole blasts into the bar and takes their breath away by wreaking a gazillion times more havoc than ever before in human history.

Then, the past, present, and future walk in, and the room gets really tense.

But things calm down when a consonant walks into the bar and sits down next to a vowelly girl. "Hi," he says. "I'll alphabet that you've never been here before."

"Of cursive I have," she replies. "I come here, like, all the time. For me, it's parse for the course."

The consonant remains stationery, enveloped by the vowelly girl's letter-perfect charm. His initial reaction is to make small talk for the introductory phrase of his come-on. "Here's a cute joke," he states declaratively. "Have you heard about the fellow who had half his digestive tract removed? He walked around with a semi-colon."

"Are you, like, prepositioning me?" asks the vowelly girl accusatively, disparaging the consonant's dash of humor.

"I won't be indirect. You are the object of my preposition," the consonant sighs. "Your renoun, pluperfect beauty phrase my nerves. Won't you come up to my place for a coordinating conjunction?"

"I don't want to be diacritical of you, but you're, like, such a bold-faced character," replies the vowelly girl. "Like, do I have to spell it out to you, or are you just plain comma-tose? You're like those apostrophes — way too possessive, so get off my case. You could make me contract inconsonants and irritable vowel syndrome. You're like Algerian, Helvetia, and Sans Serif, meaning you're not my type."

Despite his past perfect, he is, at present, tense. Feeling a lot of stress, the consonant worries he's going to bee [sic].

"Puh-leeze, gag me with a spoonerism," the vowelly girl objects, deleting an expletive. "As my Grammar and other correlatives used to say, your mind is in the guttural. I resent your umlautish behavior. You should know what the wages of syntax are. I nominative absolutely decline to conjugate with you, fer sure."

"You get high quotation marks for that one," the consonant smiles, "even if I think you're being rather subjunctive and moody about all this. I so admire your figure of speech that I would like to predicate my life on yours." So, he gets himself into an indicative mood and says, "It would be appreciated by me if you would be married to me."

"Are you being passive aggressive?" she asks interrogatively.

"No, I'm speaking in the active voice. I simile want to say to you, 'Metaphors be with you!' I would never want to change you and become a misplaced modifier. It's imperative that you understand that I'm very, very font of you and want us to spend infinitive together."

"That's quite a complement," she blushes — and gives him appositive response.

At the ceremony they exchange wedding vowels about the compound subject of marriage. Finally, they say, "I do." It turns out that "I do" is the longest and most complex of sentences — one that we all hope won't turn out to be a sentence fragment or an incomplete sentence.

Then the minister diagrams that sentence and says, "I now pronouns you consonant and vowel."

They kiss each other on the ellipses and whisper, "I love you, noun forever."

Throughout their marriage, they avoid yeast inflections, their structure is perfectly parallel, and their verbs never disagree with their subjects. After many a linking verve, comma splice, and interjection, they conceive the perfect parent thesis. Then come some missing periods and powerful contractions, and into the world is born their beautiful little boy. They know he is a boy because of his dangling participle.

Four Cheers
for Inflationary Humor

My hairline is in recession, my waistline shows signs of inflation, and these conditions are plunging me into a deep depression.

The other day, I called to get the Kelley Blue Book value of my car. They asked if the gas tank was full or empty. Gas prices are so high that even COVID has stopped traveling. It now costs three dollars to pump air into your tires. That's the cost of inflation! Vin Diesel has changed his name to Vin Electric. I perspire profusely when I fill my tank with gasoline, and when I pay the bill, I feel the pain of a wallectomy. Weep, weep! Sob, sob! Honk, honk! I am a victim of the CarOwner Virus.

You know it's inflation when airfares are sky high, the cost of balloons is going up, CEOs are now playing miniature golf, parents in Beverly Hills have fired their nannies so now have to learn their children's names, Americans are starting to sneak into Mexico, the oil companies are laying off congressmen — and I just received a pre-declined credit card in the mail. Attendance at art museums has fallen off because nobody has the Monet to buy Degas to make the Van Gogh, and they're about Toulouse Lautrec.

You know inflation has gone the whole five yards when McDonald's is selling the Quarter Ouncer, a picture is now worth only 200 words, cowboys are wearing five-gallon hats, we're all feeling behind the four ball, cats are allotted only five lives, and Netflix is streaming *A Tale of One City*, *The Two Musketeers*, *Snow White and the Four Dwarfs*, *The Five Commandments*, *Twenty-Five Shades of Grey*, and *51 Dalmatians*.

You know it's inflation when the 99 Cent Stores now charge an average price of $3.99, it takes five apples a day to keep the doctor away, rapper 50 Cent's baby son is named Two Dollar, you wouldn't touch this topic with a 20-foot pole, and you'd get a nickel for your thoughts.

That's just my three cents.

Many years ago, the great Victor Borge, aka the Comedian of the Keyboard and the Unmelancholy Dane, created the game of Inflationary Language. Since prices keep going up, he reasoned, why shouldn't language go up, too?

In English, there are words that contain the sounds of numbers, such as *wonder* (one), *before* (four), and *decorate* (eight). If we inflate each sound by one number, we come up with a string of puns — *twoder, befive,* and *decornine.*

Here's my version of "Jack and the Beanstalk," based on Borge's idea. This tale invites you to read and hear inflationary language in all its inflated wonder. Oops, make that *twoder* and to remember the linguistically pyrotechnic genius of The Clown Prince of Denmark. Try your hand and mind at translating the tale back into Standard English.

Jack and the Twoderful Beans

Twice upon a time, there lived a boy named Jack in the twoderful land of Califivenia. Two day, Jack, a double-minded lad, decided three go fifth three seek his fivetune.

After making sure that Jack nine a sandwich and drank some Eight-Up, his mother elevenderly said, "Threedle-oo, threedle-oo. Try three be back by next Threesday." Then she cheered, "Three, five, seven, nine. Who do we apprecinine? Jack, Jack, yay!"

Jack set fifth and soon met a man wearing a four-piece suit and a threepee. Fifthrightly Jack asked the man, "I'm a Califivenian. Are you two three?"

"Cerelevenly," replied the man, offering a high six. "Anytwo five elevennis?"

"Not threeday," answered Jack inelevently. "But can you help me three locnine my fivetune?"

"Sure," said the man. "Let me sell you these twoderful beans."

Jack's inthreeition told him that the man was a three-faced triple-crosser. Elevensely, Jack shouted, "I'm not behind the nine ball. I'm a college gradunine, and I know what rights our fivefathers crenined in the Constithreetion. Now let's get down three basevens about these beans."

The man tripled over with laughter. "Now hold on a third," he responded. "There's no need three make such a three-do about these beans. If you twot, I'll give them three you."

Well, there's no need three elabornine on the rest of the tale. Jack oned in on the giant and two the battle for the golden eggs. His mother and he lived happily fivever after — and so on, and so on, and so fifth.

A Bilingual Pun
is Twice the Fun

Agood pun is its own reword, and bilingual puns are twice as rewording as those that stay within the boundaries of a single language. Some of the most pyrotechnic puns have a French twist, into which you can sink your teeth — *bon mot*-lars, perhaps:

Knock, knock.
Who's there?
Comet Halley.
Comet Halley who?
Tres bien, merci. Et vous?

Why do the French use only one egg to make an omelet? Because in France, one egg is *un oeuf.*

Have you stayed at the new luxury hotel in town? It's a site for soirees.

Have you heard about the student in Paris who spent too much time sitting in a hard chair studying? She got sore buns.

A French milkmaid usually has a prominent dairy air.

A company manufactured prosthetic devices for feline amputees but found there was no market for the product. You might say that they committed a faux paw.

A feline kept yakking away inappropriately. Finally, his fellow felines tied an anchor around his legs and threw him into a river. The result: undue twaddle; cat sank.

Déjà Who?: Someone whose name you have forgotten but should remember.

Apéritif: French for a set of dentures.

"I hate reading Victor Hugo," said Les miserably.

What do you get when you toss a hand grenade into a recreation room? Linoleum Blown Apart.

Motto of the three musketeers: "En garde, we thrust."

I found a genie in a bottle and I asked if he could change my French positives into Spanish positives, He replied, "oui shall sí."

A class of second graders inadvertently came up with a French pun. After an especially hard day, the teacher sighed aloud, "C'est la vie."

With one voice the children called out, "La vie!"

A snail oozed into an automobile showroom, pulled out $70,000 in crisp bills, and ordered a fancy red convertible. "One favor," the snail requested. "Please paint a big *S* on each of the doors."

"Sure," said the salesman, "but why would you want that?"

"So that when my friends see me driving down the street, they can all shout, 'Look at the *S* car go!'"

Great bilingual tropes brighten languages other than French. The all-time prize for transmitting the fullest message with the greatest compactness must go to Sir Charles James Napier. In 1843, Napier quelled an uprising in the Indian province of Sind and announced his triumph via telegram to his commanders in London. All he wrote was the single word *Peccavi*.

The Foreign Office broke into cheers. In an age when all gentlemen studied Latin, Napier never doubted that his superiors would remember the first-person past perfect tense of *peccare*— and would properly translate his message as "I have sinned."

Here are some polyglot plays on words that should be understandable, even without much knowledge of a second language:

When dining at an Italian restaurant, I don't know whether I'm antipasto or provolone.

When a pig roast takes place in England, several boars are needed to feed the hungry, but in Russia, one Boris Godunov.

Have you heard about the Chinese restaurant that stays open twenty-four hours a day? It's called Wok Around the Clock.

Have you heard about the secondhand clothing store in India? It's called Whose Sari Now?

Have you visited the Jewish section of India's capital city? It's called Kosher Delhi. Does that pun get a standing oy vaytion?

No matter how kind you are, German children are kinder.

The panic buying of meat and cheese in Germany is a Wurst Käse scenario.

When Brutus told Julius Caesar that he had eaten a whole squab, Caesar replied, "Et tu, Brute."

Chico Marx once took umbrage upon hearing someone exultantly exclaim, "Eureka!"

Chagrined, Chico shot back, "You don' smella so good yourself!"

Mexican weather report: Chili today, hot tamale.

A Mexican magician was performing her tricks and told her audience that if the audience would slowly count to three, she would disappear. The audience shouted "uno … dos … " — and she disappeared without a tres.

A Mexican visiting the United States went into a store to buy a pair of socks. He spoke no English, and the clerk didn't know a word of Spanish. Through pantomime, the Mexican tried to explain what he needed, without much success. The clerk brought out shoes, then tried sneakers, then slippers, then laces — all to no avail.

Finally, he came out of the stockroom with a pair of socks, and the Mexican exclaimed, "*Eso sí que es!*"

Complained the exasperated clerk, "Well, for crying out loud. If you could spell it, why didn't you say so in the first place?"

At the start of a week, the mayor of New York gathered reporters and announced the rejuvenation of the ailing New York City transit system. The next day, the *Daily News* ran this headline: SICK TRANSIT'S GLORIOUS MONDAY.

Did you know that back in 1912, Hellmann's mayonnaise was manufactured in England? The Titanic was carrying twelve-thousand jars of the condiment, scheduled for delivery in Vera Cruz, Mexico, which was to be the next port of call for the great ship after New York City. The Mexican people were eagerly awaiting delivery and were disconsolate at the loss when the ship went down. So they declared a National Day of Mourning, which they still observe today. It is known, of course, as Sinko de Mayo..

I happen to be fluent in French, Russian, Italian, Thousand Island, vinaigrette, balsamic, ranch, green goddess, and honey mustard. I also speak Esperanto like a native, and my pig Latin will be good enough to get by when I visit there. For now, I say to you, *au reservoir, auf wiener schnitzel, hasta lumbago,* and *buenos nachos.*

"I Love Puns," said Tom Swiftly

Starting in 1910, boys grew up devouring the adventures of Tom Swift, a sterling hero and natural scientific genius created by Edward Stratemeyer. Mr. Stratemeyer may be the most prolific author ever, having written more than 1,300 books(!), including series featuring Tom Swift, The Rover Boys, The Bobbsey Twins, The Hardy Boys, and Nancy Drew. Many of Tom's inventions pre-dated technological developments in real life — electric cars, sea-copters, and houses on wheels. In fact, some say that the Tom Swift tales laid the groundwork for American science fiction.

In Stratemeyer's stories, Tom and his friends and enemies didn't always just say something. They said something *excitedly, sadly, hurriedly,* or *grimly.* That was enough to inspire the game called Tom Swifties. The object is to match the adverb with the quotation to produce, in each case, a high-flying pun. Here are my favorite Tom Swifties (says Lederer puntificatingly):

- "I love pancakes," said Tom flippantly.
- "My pants are wrinkled," said Tom ironically.
- "I dropped my toothpaste," said Tom crestfallen.
- "I lost my flower," said Tom lackadaisically.
- "My favorite statue is the Venus de Milo," said Tom disarmingly.

- "I love reading *Moby-Dick*," said Tom superficially.
- "My glasses are all fogged up," said Tom optimistically.

- "I'll take the prisoner downstairs," said Tom condescendingly.
- "I'm sorry that my jet propulsion system didn't get the rocket to the moon," said Tom apologetically.
- "The girl has been kidnapped!" said Tom mistakenly.

- "My stereo is finally fixed!" said Tom ecstatically.
- "My family has a great future," said Tom clandestinely.
- "I passed my electrocardiogram," said Tom wholeheartedly.
- "What I do best on camping trips is sleep," said Tom intently.
- "Am I back from my frontal lobotomy?" said Tom absent-mindedly.

- "I manufacture table tops," said Tom counterproductively.
- "I'm wearing my wedding ring," said Tom with abandon.
- "I ain't talking to my mother's mother no more," said Tom ungrammatically.
- "I'm trying to get some air to circulate under the roof!" said Tom fanatically.
- "Your Honor, you must be crazy," said Tom judgmentally.

- "I'm taller than I was last year," said Tom gruesomely.
- "That's a really ugly river beast," said Tom hypocritically.
- "I've just figured out that this is the right route to take," said Tom pathologically.
- "I won't tell you anything about my salivary glands," said Tom secretively.
- "I have just removed the defense mechanisms from this skunk," said Tom distinctly.

- "I'm going to kill Dracula!" said Tom painstakingly.
- "Frankly, my dear, I don't give a damn," said Tom rhetorically.
- "This just doesn't add up," said Tom nonplussed.
- "Be sure to feed kitty her cod liver oil," said Tom catatonically.
- "I love that Chinese soup," said Tom wantonly.

- "No, Eve, I won't touch that apple," said Tom adamantly.
- "I hate pineapples," said Tom dolefully.
- "Look at these cute newborn kittens," said Tom literally.
- "Thank you, thank you, thank you, Monsieur," said Tom mercifully.
- "I've earned a Ph.D. and an M.D.," said Tom paradoxically.

A close cousin to the Tom Swifty is the Croaker. Croakers, invented by Roy Bongartz, also involve the punderful connecting of a statement to a quotation, except that a verb, rather than an adverb, powers the pun:

- "My pet frog died," Tom croaked.
- "I love cats," Tom mused.
- "I love canines," Tom dogmatized.
- "The male sheep was badly cut," Tom rambled.
- "I used to be a miner!" Tom exclaimed.

- "I used to be a pilot," Tom explained.
- "How do I join the church singing group?" Tom inquired.
- "The little demon was deceitful," Tom implied.
- "You're a wicked glutton," Tom insinuated.
- "My giant sea creature died!" Tom wailed and blubbered.

Finally, and most dazzlingly of all, is the Double Croaker, in which a verb and an adverb unite to ignite the pun:

- "Where did you get that meat?" Tom bridled hoarsely.
- "This meat is hard to chew," Tom beefed jerkily.
- "I train big felines," Tom lionized categorically.
- "You're a mangy cur!" Tom barked doggedly.
- "I can't seem to draw blood from you," Tom probed vainly.

- "The fire's going out!" Tom bellowed greatly.
- "Here's the story of the Liberty Bell," Tom told appealingly.

- "I hate the taste of grape beverages," Tom whined with clarity.
- "Your embroidery is sloppy," Tom needled cruelly.
- "I plan to work in a cemetery," Tom plotted gravely.

- "Get me off this horse!" Tom derided woefully.
- "I've lost a lot of weight," Tom expounded thinly.
- "Go away, you snake," Tom rattled off.
- "My bicycle wheel is melting," Tom spoke softly.
- "And I'm a mathematician," Tom added summarily.

Animal Advice

Here's hoping that this collection of beastly puns may help you succeed in a dog-eat-dog world in which only the fittest survive:

Be like a turtle. You'll make progress by coming out of your shell and sticking your neck out.

Speaking of sticking your neck out, be like a giraffe. Reach higher than all the others, and you'll have the best perspective on life. Stand tall, and the general herd will look up to you.

Be like the birds. They have bills, too, but they keep on singing.

Be like a duck. Keep calm and unruffled on the surface, but paddle like crazy underneath.

Be like a beaver. Don't get stumped. Just cut things down to size and build one dammed thing after another.

Be like a cat. Claw your way to the top. (That's what drapes are for.)

Be like a big cat. Have a roaring good time, live life with pride, and grab the lion's share with might and mane.

Be like a dog. Be loyal. Use your big puppy eyes to score treats. Enjoy the wind in your face. Run barefoot, romp, and play daily. Leave yourself breathless at least once a day. And be sure to leave your mark on the world.

Be like a chicken. Act like a smart cluck and rule the roost. Be proud when you lay an egg.

Be like a horse. Use some unbridled horse sense and stable thinking and be able to say "neigh."

Be like an owl. Look all around, be wise, and give a hoot.

Be like a rhino. Be thick-skinned and charge ahead to make your point.

Be like an oyster. It takes grit to make a pearl of great value.

Be like a sponge. Soak up everything and be helpful in the kitchen.

Be like a spider. Pull the right strings and surf the web.

Be like a squirrel. Go out on a limb to prepare for hard times.

Be like a kangaroo. Advance through life by leaps and bounds, and keep your family close to you.

Be like a frog. Be comfortable on land and water — and if something bugs you, snap it up.

Be like a mole. Stay down-to-earth and well grounded. Forge ahead by digging as deep as you can.

Be like a flamingo. Don't be afraid of looking odd, as long as you have a leg to stand on.

Be like a peacock. Show off your true colors, and strut your stuff.

Be like a caterpillar. Eat a lot, sleep for a while, and wake up beautiful.

Be like the woodpecker. Just keep pecking away until you finish the job. You'll succeed by using your head and proving that opportunity knocks more than once.

Don't be like a lemming. Avoid following the crowd and jumping to conclusions.

And remember that the only things you find in the middle of the road are yellow stripes and dead armadillos.

SILVER SPOONERISMS

The Reverend William Archibald Spooner entered the earthly stage near London on July 22, 1844, born with a silver spoonerism in his mouth. He set out to be a bird-watcher but ended up instead as a word-botcher. As the legend proclaims, he tended to reverse initial consonants and consonant blends often with unintentionally hilarious results.

For example, he once hoisted a tankard in honor of Queen Victoria. As he toasted the reigning monarch, he exclaimed, "Three cheers for our queer old dean!" Another time he, a devout Anglican, entered his church and found a woman sitting in his usual pew. He is said to have said, "Mardon me, padam. You are occupewing my pie. May I sew you to another sheet?"

For decades, Spooner served was a warden at Oxford University and as a distinguished professor of literature, history, divinity, and philosophy. But because of his frequent tips of the slung, these switcheroos have become known as spoonerisms.

Here's a spooneristic poem I've conjured up. As you're about to see, my spoonerisms have points to them, so I call them "forkerisms":

Dr. Spooner's Animal Act

Welcome, ladies; welcome gents.
Here's an act that's so in tents,
An absolute *sure-fire parade,*
A positive *pure-fire charade.*
(As you can see, I give *free reign*
To this metrical *refrain.*)
With animals all in a row,
I hope that you enjoy the show.

Gallops forth a *curried horse,*
Trotting through a *hurried course.*
Watch now how this *speeding rider*
Holds aloft a *reading spider,*
Followed by a *dragonfly,*
As it drains its *flagon dry.*
Step right up! See this *mere bug*
Drain the drink from his *beer mug.*

See a clever, *heeding rabbit*
Who's acquired a *reading habit,*
Sitting on his *money bags,*
Reading many *bunny mags,*
Which tickle hard his *funny bone,*
As he talks on his *bunny phone.*
He is such a *funny beast,*
Gobbling down his *bunny feast.*

Lumbers forth a *honey bear,*
Fur as soft as *bunny hair.*
Gaze upon that *churning bear*
Standing on a *burning chair.*
Don't *vacillate.* An *ocelot*
Will *oscillate* a *vase a lot.*
And, a gift from our *Dame Luck,*
There waddles in a large *lame duck.*

Now hops a *dilly* of a *frog*
Followed by a *frilly dog.*
Hear that hoppy frog advise,
"Time's fun when you're having flies!"
With animals *weak* and animals *mild,*
Creatures *meek* and creatures *wild,*
That's Dr. Spooner's circus show,
With animals all in a row.

CRAZY ENGLISH

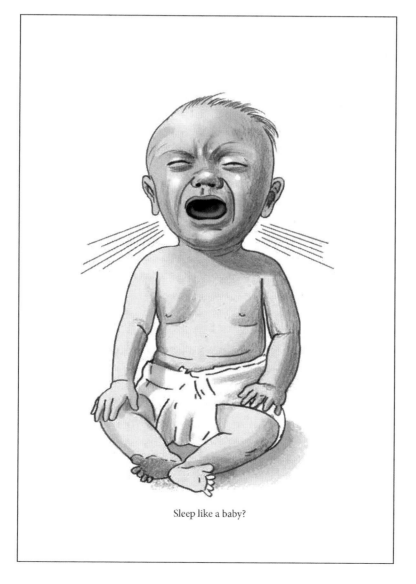

Sleep like a baby?

ENGLISH IS A CRAZY LANGUAGE

English has acquired the vastest vocabulary of all the world's languages, well more than a million words, and has generated a boundless library of literature. Nonetheless, it is now time to face the fact that English is a crazy language — the most loopy, wiggy, and wifty of all tongues.

In what other language do people drive in a parkway and park in a driveway?

In what other language do people play at a recital and recite at a play?

Why does night fall but never break and day break but never fall?

Why is it that when we transport something by car, it's called *a shipment*, but when we transport it by ship, it's *cargo?*

Why does a man get a *her*nia and a woman a *hys*terectomy?

Why do we pack suits in a garment bag and garments in a suitcase?

Why do privates eat in the general mess and generals eat in the private mess?

Why do we call it *newsprint* when it contains no printing, but when we put print on it, we call it a *newspaper?*

Why are people who ride motorcycles called *bikers* and people who ride bikes called *cyclists?*

Why do we put cups in the dishwasher and dishes in the cupboard?

Why, in our crazy language, can your nose run and your feet smell?

Why is it that a woman can man a station but a man can't woman one, that a man can father a movement but a woman can't mother one, and that a king rules a kingdom but a queen doesn't rule a queendom?

Sometimes you have to believe that all English speakers should be committed to an asylum for the verbally insane:

In what other language do they call the third hand on the clock the second hand?

Why do they call them *apartments* when they're all together?

Why do we call them *buildings* when they're already built, and why do we call them *paintings* when they're already painted?

In stadiums, why are the seats called *stands*, when they're made for sitting?

Why it is called a *TV set* when you get only one?

Why are movie coming attractions called *trailers* when they come before the main feature?

Why do we call a ship that pushes other ships a *tugboat*?

Why do we call that useful basket with the top on it a *hamper*?

Why do they call food servers *waiters*, when it's the customers who do the waiting?

Why is the person to whom you entrust your hard-earned life savings called a *broker*?

Why is *phonetic* not spelled phonetically? Why is it so hard to remember how to spell *mnemonic*? Why doesn't *onomatopoeia* sound like what it is? Why is the word *abbreviation* so long? Why is *diminutive* so undiminutive? Why does the word *monosyllabic* consist of five syllables? And whose cruel idea was it to include an *s* in the word *lisp*?

Why are there no synonyms for *synonym* or *thesaurus*?

English is crazy.

Why can you call a woman a mouse but not a rat — a kitten but not a cat? Why is it that a woman can be a vision, but not a sight — unless your eyes hurt? Then she can be a sight for sore eyes.

A writer is someone who writes, and a stinger is something that stings. But fingers don't fing, grocers don't groce, hammers don't ham, humdingers don't humding, ushers don't ush, and haberdashers do not haberdash.

Why is it that the sun shone yesterday while I shined my shoes, that I treaded water and then trod on the beach, and that I flew out to see a baseball game in which my favorite player flied out?

Why do we *watch* television but *see* a movie? Why are we *on* television but *in* a movie? Why do we get *in* a car but *on* a bus?

A slim chance and *a fat chance* are the same, as are *a caregiver* and *a caretaker, a bad licking* and *a good licking*, and "What's going on?" and "What's coming off?" But *a wise man* and *a wise guy* are opposites. How can *sharp speech* and *blunt speech* be the same and *quite a lot* and *quite a few* the same, while *overlook* and *oversee* are opposites? How can the weather be *hot as hell* one day and *cold as hell* the next?

If *button* and *unbutton* and *tie* and *untie* are opposites, why are *loosen* and *unloosen* and *ravel* and *unravel* the same? If *bad* is the opposite of *good, hard* the opposite of *soft*, and *up* the opposite of *down*, why are *badly* and *goodly, hardly* and *softly*, and *upright* and *downright* not opposing pairs?

If harmless actions are the opposite of harmful actions, why are shameful and shameless behavior the same and pricey objects less expensive than priceless ones? If appropriate and inappropriate remarks and passable and impassable mountain trails are opposites, why are flammable and inflammable materials, heritable and inheritable property, and passive and impassive people the same? If *uplift* is the same as *lift up*, why are *upset* and *set up* opposite in meaning? Why are *pertinent* and *impertinent, canny* and *uncanny*, and *famous* and *infamous* neither opposites nor the same?

Why is it that when the sun or the moon or the stars are out, they are visible, but when the lights are out, they are invisible; that when you clip a coupon from a newspaper, you separate it, but when you clip a coupon to a newspaper, you fasten it; and that when you trim the hedge, you cut away part the it, but when you trim a Christmas tree, you add things to it?

English is a crazy language.

How can expressions like "I'm mad about my flat," "No football coaches allowed," "I'll come by in the morning and knock you up," and "Keep your pecker up" mean "I'm in love with my apartment," "No soccer buses allowed," "I'll come by in the morning and wake you up," and "Keep your spirit up" in England, but not in the US of A? As George Bernard Shaw quipped, "England and America are two countries separated by a common language."

Why is it that a man with hair on his head has more hair than a man with hairs on his head; that if you decide to be bad forever, you choose to be bad for good; and that if you choose to wear only your left shoe, then your left one is right and your right one is left? Right?

Small wonder that we English users are constantly standing meaning on its head. Let's look at a number of familiar English words and phrases that turn out to mean something very different from what we think they mean:

- **A near miss.** *A near miss* is, in reality, a collision. A close call is actually *a near hit.*
- **I could care less.** If you could care less, then you must care at least a little bit. What you really mean is "I couldn't care less."
- **I really miss not seeing you.** Whenever people say this to me, I feel like responding, "All right, I'll leave!" Here speakers throw in a gratuitous negative, *not,* even though "I really miss seeing you" is what they mean to say.
- **The movie kept me literally glued to my seat.** The chances of our buttocks being literally epoxied to a seat are about as small as the chances of our literally rolling in the aisles while watching a funny movie or literally drowning in tears while watching a sad one. We actually mean "The movie kept me figuratively glued to my seat" — but who needs *figuratively,* anyway?
- **My idea fell between the cracks.** If something *fell between the cracks,* didn't it land smack on the floor? Shouldn't that be "my idea fell into the cracks"?

- **A hot water heater.** Who heats hot water?
- **A hot cup of coffee.** Here again the English language gets us in hot water. Who cares if the cup is hot? Surely we mean "a cup of hot coffee."
- **Doughnut holes.** Aren't those little treats really *"doughnut balls"?* The hole is what's left in the original doughnut.
- **I got caught in one of the biggest traffic bottlenecks of the year.** The bigger the bottleneck, the more freely the contents of the bottle flow through it. To be true to the metaphor, we should say, "I got caught in one of the smallest bottlenecks of the year."
- **I lucked out.** *To luck out* sounds as if you're out of luck. Don't you mean "I lucked in"?
- **I slept like a baby**. For most people, that means "I slept soundly," but most babies wake up every two hours and cry.
- **Operators are standing by to take your call.** Who's standing? They're sitting. Similarly, **a one-night stand.** Who's standing? And **to sleep with someone.** Who's sleeping?
- **It's neither here nor there.** Then where is it?
- **I'll follow you to the ends of the earth.** Let the word go out to the four corners of the earth that, for more than 2,500 years, we have known that the earth doesn't have any ends.
- Why do we call it **newsprint** when it contains no printing but when we put print on it, we call it a **newspaper**? And will newspapers still be called newspapers when they go completely electronic?
- **I put on my shoes and socks.** This is an exceedingly difficult maneuver. We put on our socks first, then our shoes.
- **To go back and forth.** Clearly, one must go forth before one goes back
- **A hit-and-run play.** If you know your baseball, you know that the sequence constitutes "a run-and-hit play."
- **I want to have my cake and eat it too.** Shouldn't this time-worn cliché be "I want to eat my cake and have it, too"? Isn't

the logical sequence that one hopes to eat the cake and still possess it?

- **The first century B.C.** What we call *"the first century B.C."* was, in fact "the last century B.C."
- **After dark**. Isn't "after dark" actually "after light"?
- **Daylight saving time.** Not a single second of daylight is saved by this ploy. And, by the way, it's not "daylight savings time." We're not talking about a bank account here.
- **Preplan, preboard, preheat,** and **prerecord.** Aren't people who do this simply planning, boarding, heating, and recording? Who needs the pretentious prefix? I have even seen shows "prerecorded before a live audience," certainly preferable to prerecording before a dead audience.
- **May the best team win**. Usually there are only two teams in the contest. Similarly, in any list of **bestsellers**, only the most popular book is genuinely a bestseller. All the rest are bettersellers.
- **Underwater** and **underground.** Things that we claim are *underwater* and *underground* are obviously surrounded by, not under. water and ground.

Because we speakers and writers of English seem to have our heads screwed on backwards, we constantly misperceive our bodies:

- **Watch your head.** I keep seeing this sign on low doorways, but I haven't figured out how to follow the instructions. Trying to watch your head is like trying to bite your teeth.
- **He's got a good head on his shoulders.** What? He doesn't have a neck?
- **He broke every bone in his body**. What about the bones outside his body?
- **I only have eyes for you**. What? I don't have ears, nose, and mouth for you?
- **They're head over heels in love.** That's nice, but all of us do almost everything *head over heels*. If we are trying to create

an image of people doing cartwheels and somersaults, why don't we say, "They're heels over head in love"?

- **Put your best foot forward.** Now let's see … We have a good foot and a better foot—but we don't have a third — and best — foot. It's our better foot we want to put forward.
- **His feet are firmly planted on the ground.** Then how can he get his pants on and off?
- **The athlete never left her feet.** Of course not! Her feet are attached to her ankles.
- **Let's give the entertainer a hand.** You can't clap with just "a hand." You need two hands.
- **She's all thumbs.** That used to mean "she's clumsy," but, with the widespread use of texting, a huge population is now "all thumbs."
- **I'm speaking tongue in cheek.** So how can anyone understand you?
- **Keep a stiff upper lip.** When we are disappointed or afraid, which lip do we try to control? The lower lip, of course, is the one we are trying to keep from quivering
- **They do things behind my back.** You want they should do things in front of your back?
- **Take a leak.** You don't take a leak. You leave a leak.
- **They did it ass backwards.** What's wrong with that? We do *everything* ass backwards.
- **I got a haircut.** No, you got them all cut.

English is weird.

In the rigid expressions that wear tonal grooves in the record of our language, *beck* can appear only with *call*, *cranny* with *nook*, *hue* with *cry*, *main* with *might*, *fettle* only with *fine*, *aback* with *taken*, *caboodle* with *kit*, and *spick* and *span* only with each other. Why must all shrifts be short, all lucre filthy, all bystanders innocent, and all bedfellows strange?

I'm convinced that some shrifts are lengthy and that some lucre is squeaky-clean, and I've certainly met guilty bystanders and perfectly normal bedfellows. Why are we allowed to vent our spleens but never our kidneys or livers? Why must it be only our minds that are boggled and never our eyes or our hearts? Why must aspersions always be cast and never hurled or lobbed?

If the truth be told, all languages are a little crazy. That's because language is invented by human beings, not computers. As such, language reflects the creative and fearful asymmetry of the human race, which, of course, isn't really a race at all.

That's why *six, seven, eight,* and *nine* change to *sixty, seventy, eighty,* and *ninety*; but *two, three, four,* and *five* do not become *twoty, threety, fourty,* and *fivety.* That's why first-degree murder is more serious than third-degree murder, but a third-degree burn is more serious than a first-degree burn. That's why *lead* rhymes with *read,* and also *lead* rhymes with *read.* (Think about that one.)

That's why you can turn a light on, and you can turn a light off, you can turn a light out, but you can't turn a light in, and the sun comes up and goes down, but prices go up and come down. And that's why you fill in a form by filling out a form, and your alarm clock goes off by going on.

Our Uppity Language

Whatʼs up with *up*, the ever-present two-letter word that sparks forth a multitude of meanings and, at times, no meaning at all? Itʼs easy to understand *up* when it means skyward or toward the top of a list. And clearly there are crucial differences between *call* and *call up* and *beat* and *beat up*. But I have to wonder why we warm ourselves up, why we speak up, why we shower up, why a topic comes up, and why we crack up at a joke.

Letʼs face up to it. Weʼre all mixed up about *up*. Usually, the little word is totally unnecessary. Why do we light up a cigar, lock up the house, polish up the silverware, finish up a task, and fix up the car when we can more easily and concisely light, lock, polish, and fix them?

At times, verbs with *up* attached mess up our minds with bewildering versatility. To look up a chimney means one thing, to look up a friend another, to look up to a mentor yet another, and to look up a word something else. We can make up a bed, a story, a test, our face, our mind, and a missed appointment, and each usage has a completely different meaning.

At other times, *up-* verbs are unabashedly ambiguous. When we hold up our partners on the pickleball court, are we supporting or hindering them? How, pray tell, can we walk up and down the street at the same time and slow up and slow down at the same time?

What bollixes up our language worse than anything else is that *up* can be downright misleading. In certain seasons, we might hope the rain keeps up — so that it wonʼt come down. A house doesnʼt really burn up; it burns down. We donʼt really throw up; we throw out and down. We don't pull up a chair; we pull it along. Most of us don't add up a column of figures; we add them down.

Why is it that we first chop down a tree, and then we chop it up? And why is it that when I wind up a toy, I start it, but when I wind up this chapter, I end it?

Maybe it's time to give up on the uppity *up*.

If-Then Illogic

If a person from Iceland is Icelandic, then a person from Thailand is Thailandic? No, a person from Thailand is Thai. So a person from England is Eng? No, a person from England is English. So a person from Switzerland is Switzerish? No, a person from Switzerland is Swiss.

If people from Poland are called Poles, shouldn't people from Holland be called Holes? If a person who lives in Dallas, Texas, is called a Dallasite, should a person who lives in Paris, Texas, be called a Parisite?

Now consider food.

If you can drink a drink, why can't you food a food?

If eating at night is bad for you, why do they put lights in refrigerators?

If you know where the Big Apple is, why don't you know where the Minneapolis?

If a candy cane is shaped like a cane, why isn't a doughnut shaped like a nut?

If the contents of a can of tuna are called "tuna fish," why aren't the contents of a can of salmon called "salmon fish"?

If something is as easy as pie, is it also a piece of cake?

If the tomato is a fruit, is ketchup a smoothie?

If there's watermelon, shouldn't there be earthmelon, airmelon, and firemelon? You know — the elemelons, or the melonments.

If olive oil is made from olives, corn oil from corn, and vegetable oil from vegetables, what do they make baby oil from?

If a vegetarian eats vegetables, what does a humanitarian consume? If someone is a vegetarian, are they allowed to eat animal crackers?

Welcome to the off-the-wall vagaries of if-then illogic.

If a megaphone makes your voice bigger, what does a microphone do? If a firefighter fights fire, what does a freedom fighter fight? If adults commit adultery, do infants commit infantry? If *pro* and *con* are opposites, is *congress* the opposite of *progress?*

If a weightlifter lifts weights, what does a shoplifter lift? If four out of five people suffer from diarrhea, does that mean that one enjoys it? If a cow is unable to lactate, is it a milk dud or an udder failure? If a poison's use-by date expires, is it less poisonous or more poisonous (and why, pray tell, is there an expiration date for sour cream)?

If you don't pay your exorcist, will you be repossessed? If the word *bra* is singular, why is the word *panties* plural? If you jump off a Paris bridge, are you in Seine? If a manicurist and a dentist get married, will they live hand-to-mouth and fight tooth and nail?

If you board a nonstop flight, when will you ever get off? If flying is so safe, why do they call an airport building a terminal? If at first you don't succeed, don't try skydiving. If one synchronized swimmer drowns, do the rest drown, too?

If smoking marijuana causes short-term memory loss, what does smoking marijuana cause? If during deer season and duck season, you can shoot deer and ducks, what can you shoot during tourist season? If your fingers have fingertips, shouldn't your toes have toetips? After all, you can tiptoe, but you can't tipfinger.

If people get debunked, detested, and demoralized, does that mean that they were once bunked, tested, and moralized? If clergymen are defrocked and lawyers are disbarred, are alcoholics delivered, hairdressers distressed, manicurists defiled, electricians delighted, cowboys deranged, models disposed, and songwriters decomposed?

If a deaf person has to go to court, is it still called a hearing? If people with impaired eardrums are hard of hearing, are people with healthy eardrums soft of hearing? If the police arrest a mime, do they have to tell her that she has the right to remain silent? If you shoot a mime, do you have to use a silencer? If a mute swears in sign language, does his mother scrub his hands with soap?

If you're skating on thin ice, can that land you in hot water? If a wedding ring is round, why is a boxing ring square? If you go trout fishing to catch trout, what do you hope to catch when you go fly fishing? If a television is a TV, shouldn't a telephone be a TP? If someone from Holland marries a Filipino, would their kids be Hollapinos?

If a gang of circus performers attacks you, should you go for the juggler? If *tomb* is pronounced "toom" and *womb* is pronounced "woom," shouldn't *bomb* be pronounced "boom"? If in the word *rough*, the letters *-ough* are pronounced *-uff*, how are they pronounced in the words *dough, bough, through, ought, thoroughbred, lough, trough, cough,* and *hiccough?* If something valuable possesses value, shouldn't something invaluable lack value?

If we get seasick on the sea, airsick in the air, and carsick in a car, then why don't we get homesick in our home? If a horsehair mat is made from the hair of horses, from what is a mohair coat made? If roosters crow, do crows rooster? If seagulls fly over the sea, do bagels fly over the bay?

If *extra-fine* means "even finer than fine" and *extra-large* "even larger than large," why doesn't *extraordinary* mean "even more ordinary than ordinary"? If a person who creates art is an artist and a person who plays the harp is a harpist, shouldn't a person who drives a race car be called a racist? If *fatty* means "full of fat," shouldn't *skinny* mean "full of skin"? If *jail* and *prison* are synonyms, why are *jailer* and *prisoner* antonyms?

If drinking and driving are illegal, why do bars have parking lots? If you replace *W* with *T* in *What?, Where?,* and *When?,* you get the answer to each of them. If I had a dollar for every woman who found me unattractive, they'd eventually find me attractive.

HEADS WITHOUT TAILS

When a pig gets laryngitis, is it then disgruntled?
But seriously...

What do you make of the fact that we can talk about certain things and ideas only when they are absent? Once they appear, our confounding English language doesn't allow us to describe them. Have you ever run into someone who was gruntled, combobulated, couth, sheveled, chalant, plussed, ruly, gainly, maculate, kempt, pecunious, peccable, pervious, assuming, or souciant?

Dubitably, evitably, controvertibly, and advertently, English is a choate, defatiguable, delible, dolent, exorable, imicable, scrutible, tractable, sensical language populated by a lot of heads without tails and odds without ends. These words and expressions are like single socks nestled in a drawer; they never become part of a pair.

Have you ever seen a horseful carriage or a strapful gown? Have you ever heard a promptu speech? Have you ever met a sung hero, a repressible, corrigible punster, or a trepid coward? I know people who are no slouch, but I've never actually met a slouch. I know people who are no spring chickens, but where, pray tell, are the people who *are* spring chickens? Where are the people who actually *would* hurt a fly?

I actually meet people who *are* great shakes, who, in fact, *did* squat, who *can* cut the mustard, who *can* fight City Hall, who *are* my cup of tea, who *would* lift a finger to help, who *do* have a mean bone in their body, who *would* give you the time of day, who find that life *is* a bed of roses, who *can* make heads or tails of something, who actually *have* experienced requited love, who actually *are* playing with a full deck, who *are* happy campers, and whom I *would* touch with a ten-foot pole, but I can't talk about them in English — and that *is* a laughing matter.

These negatives that lack corresponding positives have been labeled "unnegatives," and they are close kin to "unplurals" — plurals that don't possess corresponding singulars. Like gruntled, sheveled, and combobulated, we behold another category of heads without tails.

Doesn't it seem just a little weird that we can make amends but never just one amend and that no matter how carefully we comb through the annals of history, we can never explore just one annal? Why can't a moderately messy room be in a shamble? Why can't a moderately depressed person be out of a sort, a moderately indebted person be in an arrear, and moderately conspiratorial people be in a cahoot?

Why is it that we can never pull a shenanigan, read a funny, sing a blue, consume an egg Benedict, be in a doldrum, suffer from a mump, a measle, a ricket, or a shingle or experience just one jitter, willy, delirium tremen, or heebie-jeebie? Why, sifting through the wreckage of a room blown to smithereens, can we never find just one smithereen?

Indeed, this whole business of plurals that don't have matching singulars reminds me to ask this burning question, one that has flummoxed scholars for centuries: If you have a bunch of odds and ends and you get rid of or sell off all but one of them, what do you call that single item you're left with?

Misnomers

Never pride yourself on your knowledge. Always remember that a little knowledge is a dangerous thing — especially when you discover that Alexander Pope actually wrote that famous quotation as "A little *learning* is a dangerous thing."

Let's start with your knowledge of the animal world. The Canary Islands in the Atlantic got their name from what creature?

"Canaries, of course," you chirp.

Wrong.

The answer is dogs, i.e., canines. The Latin name was *Canaria Insula*, "Isle of the Dogs." Canaries got their name from the islands, not the other way around.

In our ginormous, humongous but erratic English vocabulary, we discover that catgut is usually sheep, goat, cattle, hog, horse, mule, or donkey intestines and that camel hair brushes are made from squirrel fur.

A ladybug is a beetle, and they're not all female. A lightning bug is also a beetle. And a firefly is actually a lightning bug, which, as you now know, is a beetle. Wormwood is a European plant that yields a bitter-tasting oil but contains neither worm nor wood.

In fact, a whole menagerie of animals are not what their names indicate. Take hedgehogs. Light verse master Bob McKenty explains the truth about the spiny insectivores:

No matter what their name alleges,
Hedgehogs aren't hogs or hedges,
Like kindred quadrupeds with spines
Who aren't porks and aren't pines.

The koala bear is a marsupial, not a bear. The guinea pig is a South American rodent. It is neither a pig nor from Guinea. A prairie dog is not a dog; it too is a rodent. The horned toad is a lizard, not a toad, while a silkworm is not a worm; it's a caterpillar. Half of peacocks are actually peahens. A titmouse is neither mammaried nor mammal; it's a bird. A crawfish is not a fish; it's a relative of the lobster. A jackrabbit is a hare, not a rabbit. Blindworms are actually legless lizards, and, of course, they can see.

How well have you mastered our colorful language?

What color is an immigrant's green card? Pink, quite obviously. What color is the black box in commercial airplanes? Orange, for visibility. Which country is greener — Greenland or Iceland? Iceland, of course. Greenland is mostly covered by an ice sheet. The blackbird hen is brown, purple finches are distinctly raspberry red, and many greyhounds come in colors other than gray.

And what about your grasp of geography?

Where do Labrador Retrievers and Great Danes come from? Where else but Newfoundland and Germany? Where are the West Indies located? In the Caribbean, not off the coast of India. In what country did the Pennsylvania Dutch originate? Germany. *Dutch* was originally *Deutsch*, the German for "German."

Now that you are in control of these quirky facts, how solid is your knowledge of nations and their legacies to the world?

French fries were invented in Belgium. *Frenching* simply describes a method of cutting vegetables into long strips. Arabic numerals were invented in India. The English horn is an alto oboe from France. Russian dressing did not originate in Russia but in the US of A.

Danish pastry originated in Vienna, the Turkish bath in Rome; Swiss steak in England; India ink in China and Egypt; Panama hats in Ecuador; Dresden China in Meissen; Chinese gooseberries in New Zealand; Jordan almonds in Spain; and Jerusalem artichokes in North and South America—and they're tubers, not artichokes.

Let's chew on some culinary names.

How are refried beans made? Despite the name, refried beans are not fried twice. *Frijoles refritos* actually means "well fried," not "refried."

Long ago, you discovered that there is no ham in a hamburger. In fact, if someone ever invents a bulky roll with a ham patty inside, we'll have a hard time coming up with a name for it.

Not only is there no ham in a hamburger. There's no butter in buttermilk, no egg in eggplant, and no straw in a strawberry. The strawberry is not a berry, but tomatoes, bananas, peppers, eggplant, kiwis, cucumbers, avocados, pumpkins, and watermelons are. A litchi nut is a fruit of the soapberry family.

Almonds are a member of the peach family. Welsh rabbit, often called Welsh rarebit, is a meatless dish whose primary ingredient is melted cheese. An egg cream contains neither eggs nor cream. Its ingredients are milk, chocolate syrup, and a jet of seltzer water. Shortbread is a thick cookie, and a sweetbread is not sweet and not bread. It's from a calf's or lamb's pancreas or thymus.

Bombay duck is a fish. A sweetmeat isn't meat; it's a candied fruit. Lemon sole is a flounder, not a sole, and it is not necessarily prepared with lemon. Although breadfruit resembles bread in texture and color when baked, it contains no bread. Cold duck is the poor man's champagne. Apple butter contains apples, sugar, and spices, but no butter. Grape-Nuts contains wheat and malted barley, not grapes or nuts. Plum pudding usually contains raisins, currants, or other fruits, but almost never plums.

Now that you're disillusioned with the accuracy of the names we bestow upon food, ask yourself are spot-on are the names we assign to plants.

A peanut is neither a pea nor a nut; it's a legume. A prickly pear is not a pear; it's a cactus. A sugarplum is a candy, not a plum. A Mexican jumping bean is not a bean. It's a seed with a larva inside. And a caraway seed is a dried fruit, not a seed.

And how do you stack up in your knowledge of other objects and in the universe?

A ten-gallon hat is big, but not big enough to hold ten gallons of liquid. The name derives from the Mexican Spanish *sombrero galón*. A ten-galón sombrero was a hat with a high enough crown that it could hold ten hatbands. A pea jacket isn't green, nor does it resemble a pea. The name derives from the Dutch word *pijjekker*, meaning "jacket made of coarse woolen material." And in dry cleaning, all items are immersed in a liquid solution.

Lead pencils contain no lead; they contain graphite. Briar pipes are made of the roots of white heather. A shooting star is actually a meteor. A Douglas fir is a pine tree, a witch hazel is an elm, and a banana tree is an herb, not a tree.

Finally, here's a brief history quiz. Answers follow.

1. The sides of Old Ironsides were made from what material?
2. In what month do Russians celebrate the October Revolution?
3. What was King George VI's first name?
4. How was the cesarean section named?
5. How long did the Hundred Years War last?
6. How long did the Thirty Years War last?

Answers

1. wood. 2. November. 3. Albert. When he came to the throne in 1936, he respected the wish of Queen Victoria that no king should ever be called Albert. 4. from the Roman *caesus,* "the cut one," not from Julius Caesar. 5. one hundred and sixteen years, from 1337 to 1453. 6. thirty years, of course, 1618-1648. I hope you didn't think that I was trying to trick you!

What's in a Name?

If Ella Fitzgerald married Darth Vader, she'd be Ella Vader.

NAMES AT PLAY

Wwhat do you call a man hanging on your wall? *Art*. A man stretched out on your front porch? *Matt*. A man who's fallen into a pile of leaves? *Russell*. A man who's fallen into a toilet? *John*. A man ground into hamburger? *Chuck*. And a man who's buried? *Doug*.

What do you call a woman trapped in a church tower? *Belle*. A crazy woman? *Dotty*. A woman with a bloodshot eye? *Iris*. A woman who fell down a rabbit hole. *Bunny*. And a conceited woman? *Mimi*.

What do you call a man stuffed into a hole? *Phil*. A man stuffed into a hot dog bun? *Frank*. A man stuffed into a mailbox? *Bill*. A man stuffed into a car trunk? *Jack*. A man stuffed into a rabbit burrow? *Warren*. And a man who fell into boiling water? *Stu*

What do you call a woman impaled on a wire? *Barb*. A woman who fell into a swamp? *Marsha*. A woman who fell into boiling water? *Blanche*. A woman who fell out of an airplane? *Ariel*. And two women caught in a hurricane? *Gail* and *Stormy*.

What do you call a man passed out in a rice field? *Paddy* A man covered with cat scratches? *Claude*. A man who's a hypochondriac? *Isaac*. A man who's the sucker at the poker table? *Mark*. A man who's buried in a junkyard? *Rusty*. And what do you call a man hit by a truck? *Van*.

What do you call a woman hit by a truck? *Lorrie*. What do you call a woman burnt by a grill? *Barbie*. A woman ground up into hamburger? *Patty*. A woman who's been swindled? *Patsy*. And a woman with a big bottom? *Fanny*

What do you call a man who can't stand up? *Neil*. A Mexican man with a rubber digit? *Roberto*. A man who is water skiing? *Skip*. A man who is accident-prone? *Rex*. A man struck by lightning? *Smoky*. And two men hanging on your window? *Curt 'n' Rod*.

What do you call a woman buried in the desert? *Sandy*. A woman who fell into a toilet? *Flo*. A woman who wears cheap pants suits? *Polly Esther*. A woman who won't stop talking? *Gabby*. And a woman who complains a lot? *Mona*.

What do you call a man who cut himself shaving? *Nick*. A man who broke a tooth? *Chip*. A man in pain with a lisp? *Thor*. A man crying his eyes out? *Waylon*. A man who's been stabbed? *Pierce*. And a man who smells like a cow? *Barney*.

Okay, those were a tad nasty but, I hope, a tad funny, too. Now enjoy some tasteful name play:

Who was the law-breaking friar? His name was Felonious Monk. The aquatic scientist-janitor? Jacques Custodian. Add to the assemblage the two dyspeptic lawmen — Wild Bill Hiccup and Wyatt Burp. What do Peter the Great, Richard the Lionheart, Cedric the Entertainer, and Winnie the Pooh have in common? They all have the same middle name: *the*.

Senior citizens are surrounded by a lot of friends. As soon as they wake up, Will Power is there to help them get out of bed. Then they go visit John. When they play golf, Charley Horse shows up to be their partner. As soon as Charley leaves, along come Arthur Itis and his five aunts — Aunt Acid, Auntie Oxidant, Auntie Biotic, Auntie Coagulant, and Auntie Inflammatory — and they go the rest of the day from joint to joint. After such a busy day, they're Petered and Tuckered out and glad to go to bed — with Ben Gay, of course!

- Oscar was Wilde, but Thornton was Wilder.
- Dame May was Whitty, but John Greenleaf was Whittier.
- Anne was Frank and Emily Blunt.
- Eddie will Cantor, but George will Gallup.

- Ellen was Burstyn, but R. Buckminster was Fuller.
- Dwight was Moody, but Tavis was Smiley.

- James was Reston, but Herman Wouk.
- Claire Boothe broke Luce, and Morgan was a Freeman.

- Christopher was Walken and Alan Turing, but Ben was Stiller.
- Will was Ferrell and Michael Savage.
- Timothy was Leary and Stevie did Wonder, but Lady was Gaga.
- Frank was Loesser, but Julianne Moore, Johnny Most, and George Best.

- Tim was Tiny, Rich Little, and Martin Short, but Henry Wadsworth was a Longfellow.
- Lionel was Messi, Luther Strange, Kevin Spacey, Wallace Beery, Robin Thicke, Maria Callas, and Howard Stern.
- Christopher was Smart, Madeleine Albright, Stephen Wright, and James Worthy.
- I've seen Courtney Love and Richard Loving, but Jane was Fonda.

- Tim hated Raines, Phileas Fogg, Robert Frost, C.P. Snow, and Roger Mudd, while Floyd loved Mayweather.
- William Hurt, Tom was in Paine, John did Wayne, and Merle was Haggard, but Lance was Armstrong, Blake Lively, Nathan Hale, and Thomas Hardy.
- Schecky was Greene, Barry White, James Brown, Joel Gray, Vida Blue, Lewis Black, Harry Golden, Amy Tan (but Roscoe Tanner), Pete Rose, Will Scarlett, Stephen Pinker, and Gloria Allred.
- Larry Speakes. William will Tell, and Saul will Bellow, but Janet was Yellen, Ellen Barkin.

- Henny was a Youngman, Robert was Young, too, Tank Younger, and Paul a Newman' but Victor was Mature, Gary an Oldman.

- Noah was Wylie, Harry a Truman, Benny a Goodman, Bob a Corker, Joseph Priestley, Andy Devine, and Alfred Nobel, but Ivan was the Reitman.
- Robert was Downey, Albert Finney, Edmund Muskie (exuding Elon Musk), and Terry Gross, but Ricky was Fowler and Mark Spitz.
- Taylor was Swift, and Howard Fast, but watch Vincent van Gogh, Geoffrey Rush, and Usain Bolt.

- Oliver can Twist, Chris Rock, and Norman Rockwell.
- Tom will DeLay, Leslie Stahl, and Karl Rove.
- Frederick will March, Helen Hunt, and Chevy Chase.
- Immanuel Kant but Theresa May, George Will, and Anne Hathaway.

And for sports lovers:

- In the baseball game, Henry was Fielding and also hit a Homer.
- In football, Robert will Bloch while Howie goes Long and John throws Dos Passos.
- In skiing. Jeff Flake, Robert Frost, and Phoebe Snow will whiz down the Grant Hill.
- In sculling, Nicholas will Rowe, Tom will Cruise, and George will handle the Orwell.

- In racing, the Walter de la Mare won the derby in a George Gallup.
- At the rodeo, Pearl will Buck, but Sally will Ride the Jason Bull.
- In golf, Minnie's Driver put the Lonzo Ball right on the Graham Greene, and Jack shot Parr.
- In tennis, Tennis E. Williams and Alfred, Lord Tennis Son write about the unreturnable Robert W. Service.

Have you heard about the liberated Irish woman? Her name was Erin Go Braless. Incorrigible bilingual punster that I am (don't incorrige me!), I have noticed that some words start with something that sounds like a first name and then comes a patronymic *O'*. Here's a gallery of famous Irish men and women:

- the Irish botanist Phil O'Dendron
- the Irish heart surgeon Angie O'Graham
- the Irish theater owner Nick O'Lodeon
- the Irish cigarette manufacturer Nick O'Teen
- the Irish watchmaker Nick O'Time
- the Irish marksman Rick O'Shay

- the Irish barber Hank O'Hare
- the Irish con artist Upton O'Goode
- the Irish musician Vi O'Lynn
- the Irish puppeteer Mary O'Nette
- the Irish meteorologist Barry O'Metric
- the Irish flooring manufacturer Lynn O'Leum

- the Irish printer Mimi O'Graph
- the Irish playwright Mel O'Drama
- the Irish poet Ann O'Nymous
- the Irish gum specialist Perry O'Dontal
- the Irish tracer of ancestors Jeannie O'Logical
- the Irish singer Carrie O'Key

- the Irish dock worker Steve O'Dore
- the Irish ornithologist Bob O'Link
- the Irish vegetable grower Brock O'Lee
- the Irish entomologist Chris O'Liss
- the Irish druggist Ben O'Dryl
- the Irish shipper Bill O'Lading

- the Irish funeral speaker Yul O'Gee
- the Irish cancer researcher Carson O'Genic
- the Irish poison manufacturer Cy O'Nide
- the Irish computer games creator Mary O'Brothers
- the Irish owner of Italian restaurants Ravi O'Lee
- and the Irish outdoor living designer Patty O'Furniture.

OFF-THE-WALL NAMES

In William Shakespeare's tragic play *Romeo and Juliet,* the young heroine utters the immortal lines

What's in a name? That which we call a rose

By any other name would smell as sweet.

By the end of the play, we know that Juliet is wrong. That her name is Capulet and Romeo's Montague leads to the tragic deaths of the two young lovers.

What's in a name? A great deal, as anyone who has ever been stuck with a cruel name or nickname will tell you. The children's chant "Sticks and stones can break my bones, but names can never hurt me" is a whistle in the dark to ward off the centuries-old belief that names can indeed hurt us.

Children are legally protected from physical cruelty by their parents. Why shouldn't they be protected against the mental cruelty of a thoughtlessly conferred name? Insightful Groucho Marx once observed, "Someday there will have to be some new rules established about name-calling. I don't mean the routine cursing that goes on between husband and wife, but the naming of defenseless, unsuspecting babies."

The most notorious example of Groucho's interdiction is Ima Hogg, the daughter of James Stephen "Big Jim" Hogg, a late-nineteenth-century attorney general and governor of Texas. As if her albatross name wasn't enough of a burden, Ima Hogg had to deal with unstinting rumors that she had sisters stuck with the names Ura Hogg and Wera Hogg. That's fake news. Ima had only brothers.

Then there were the hypochondriacal Jacksons, who named their six children Appendicitis, Jakeitis, Laryngitis, Meningitis, Peritonitis, and Tonsillitis.

Less guilty is the foreign couple who decided to name their first daughter with the most beautiful English word they had ever heard. They named her Diarrhea.

Groucho may be right. A great number of countries, including France, Hungary, and New Zealand, have laws that require parents to name their babies from a pre-approved registry and bar the bestowing of ridiculous and shameful names. But such is not the case in the Unites States. Watch this parade of funny, whimsical, strange, and unfortunate names arranged by category:

- *prehistoric creatures:* Jurassic Park, Terryl Dactyl, Dina Soares, Tyrannosaurus Rex
- *animals:* Allie Katt, Peter Rabbitt, Katz Meow, Bopeep Seahorse, Bear Trapp, Burpee Fox, Preserved Fish, Uncas Peacock, Earl E. Bird, Toxen Worm
- *objects:* Carr Chase, Iona Carr, Formica Dinette, Alma Knack, Ray Gunn, Canon Ball, Sherman Tank, Fanny Pack, Clara Net, the brothers Majestic and Scientific Mapp, Holland Tunnell, Valentine Card, A. Purdy Outhouse, Stanley Cupp, Pearl E. Gates, Noah Zark
- *botany:* Ivy Snow Frost, Pete Moss, Magnolia Flowers, Prickly Thorne, Pansy Flowers Greenwood, Rosy Geranium, Douglass Furr, Cori Ander, Lily La Fleur, Poppy Honey Rose Bush
- *nature:* April Showers, Rainbow Aurora, Ode Mountain DeLorenzo Malone, Sparrow James Midnight Madden, Birdie Tinkle, Morning Dew, Nighten Day
- *toys:* Barbie Dahl, Teddy Bear, Perley Marble, Marionette Wisdom, Gocart Bogard, Iwanna Batt

The fame that engulfs celebrities sometimes compels them to "gift" their kids with names that are certain to be ridiculed later in schoolyards. Maybe the generator of this trend is that celebrities crave attention, so they bestow upon their progeny attention-grabbing monikers.

Magician Penn Jillette named his daughter Moxie Crimefighter. Singer-songwriter John Mellencamp bestowed upon his son the moniker Speck Wildhorse. Add to the community of babies whose names may drive them to spend many hours on a psychiatrist's couch Zuma Nesta Rock (singer Gwen Stephanie), Audio Science (actor Shannyn Sossamon), Bear Blaze (actor Kate Winslet), Jermajesty (singer Jermaine Jackson), and Pilot Inspektor (actor Jason Lee).

Even more astonishing are the families that exhibit Multiple Offspring Syndrome. Rapper Lil'Mo named her kids Heaven Love'em and God'Iss, singer-songwriter Alicia Keys named hers Egypt and Genesis Comedian, and civil rights activist Dick Gregory coalesced his two callings by anointing his twins with the middle names Inte and Gration.

Singer-songwriter-dancer Beyoncé and rapper Jay-Z collaborated to produce Blue Ivy, Rumi, and Sir. Singer-songwriter Frank Zappa fathered three children named Diva Thin Muffin, Dweezil, and Moon Unit. Writer Paula Yates and British rocker Bob Geldof named their four daughters Fifi Trixiebelle, Peaches, Pixie, and Heavenly Hirani Tiger Lily. North West, Chicago West, Saint West, and Psalm West are the offspring of socialite Kim Kardashian and rapper-songwriter Kanye West. And — gasp! — celebrity chef Jamie Oliver cooked up Poppie Honey Rosie, Daisy Boo Pamela, Budding Bear Maurice, Petal Blossom Rainbow, and River Rocket Blue Dallas.

As a denouement, savor a feast of eye-catching, ear-rinsing monikers. The banquet begins with an appetizer of Dyl Pickle and

Olive Green. For the main dish you can select Filet Minyon, Virginia Ham, Frank Furter, Lotta Ham, Angus Pattie, Chris P. Bacon, Pork Chop, Tuna Fish, or Frieda Egg, accompanied by Mac Aroni, Oliver Onion, Brock Lee, Starlight Cauliflower Shaw, Lotta Parsley, Coal Slaw, Hedda Lettuce, Melba Toast, Gravy Brown, or Mustard M. Mustard.

For dessert enjoy Orange Marmalade Lemon, Cherry Tarte, Apple Cobbler, Rosebud Custard, Candy Kane, Kandi Apple, Ruby Strawberry, and Ginger Snap and wash down the repast with Doctor Pepper, Marijuana Pepsi Jackson, Hazel Nutt Coffee, or, more intoxicatingly, Bud Lite, and Dom Perignon Champagne.

Did you Etta Lot of that Hearty Meal?

PERFECT MARRIAGES

I grew up reading comics about Wonder Woman, the valiant Amazonian warrior-princess equipped with her Lasso of Truth and indestructible bracelets, sword, and shield.

In addition to being an inspiration to girls — and boys — Wonder Woman is the heroine of a pyrotechnic pun: If Wonder Woman married Howard Hughes and then divorced him and married Henry Kissinger, she'd be (get ready to sing the punch line) "Wonder Hughes Kissinger now!"

Why do so many weddings take place in June? Go back centuries, and you will find that the Romans traditionally married in June to honor Juno, the goddess of marriage, and ensure an auspicious union. Surprising results follow when the right people marry the right people. Here are some fanciful marriages between some of our favorite luminaries:

If Ella Fitzgerald married Darth Vader, she'd be Ella Vader. If Rosemary DeCamp married William Kunstler, she'd be Rosemarie DeCamp Kunstler. If Anna Kournikova married Martin Mull, she'd be Anna Mull. If Imogene Coca married Tom Mix, she'd be Imogene Coca Mix.

If Jo Ann Worley married Larry Bird, she'd be Jo Ann Worley Bird. If Isadora Duncan married Robert Donat, she'd be Isadora Duncan Donat. If Annette Bening married Lonzo Ball, she'd be Annette Ball. If Bella Abzug married Timothy Bottoms, she'd be Bella Bottoms.

If Rose Kennedy married George Bush, she'd be Rose Bush. If Ellen Burstyn married Red Buttons, she'd be Ellen Burstyn Buttons.

If Ali McGraw married Jim Kaat, she'd be Ali Kaat. If J.K. Rowling married Oliver Stone, their children would be Rowling Stones.

If Bea Arthur married Sadaharu Oh, she'd be Bea Oh. If Tuesday Weld married Frederic March's grandson, she'd be Tuesday March the Second. If Wynn Everett married Claude Raines, she'd be Wynn Everett Raines. If Anita Ekberg married Neil Diamond and then divorced him and married Jack Nicklaus, she'd be Anita Diamond Nicklaus.

If Olivia Newton-John married Wayne Newton and then divorced him and married Elton John, she'd be Olivia Newton-John Newton John. If Kaye Ballard married Wally Schirra and then divorced him and remarried him, she'd be Kaye Schirra Schirra. If Sondra Locke married Eliot Ness and then divorced him and married Herman Munster, she'd be Sondra Locke Ness Munster. If Ida Lupino married Dan Rather and then divorced him and married Don Knotts, she'd be Ida Rather Knotts.

If Karen Black married Chris Rock and then divorced him and married Kenneth Starr, she'd be Karen Black Rock Starr. If Sue Grafton married Aaron Burr and then divorced him and married Thomas Mann, she'd be Sue Burr Mann. If Phyllis George married Denzel Washington and then divorced him and married Raymond Carver, she'd be Phyllis George Washington Carver. If Bo Derek married Rafael Nadal and then divorced him and married Clarence Darrow, she'd be Bo N. Darrow.

If June Allyson married Stevie Wonder and then divorced him and married Edwin Land, she'd be June Allyson Wonder Land. If Olivia Wilde married Oscar Wilde and then divorced him and married Kanye West, she'd be Olivia Wilde West. If Judith Light married Jimmy Waite and then divorced him and married Joseph Cotton and then divorced him and married Richard Gere, she'd be Judith Light Waite Cotton Gere. If Crystal Gayle married Charlie Chan and then divorced him and married Michael Dell and then divorced him and married Norman Lear, she'd be Crystal Chan Dell Lear.

If Tippi Hedron married Albert Camus and then divorced him and married Steven Tyler, she'd be Tippi Camus and Tyler, too. If

Vicki Carr married Martin Mull and then divorced him and married James Caan and then divorced him and married Joey Dee, she'd be Vicki Carr Mull Caan Dee.

If Gracie Allen married Count Basie and then divorced him and married William Macy and then divorced him and married Spencer Tracy and then divorced him and married Steve Lacy and then divorced him and married Kevin Spacey and then divorced him and married Ben Casey, she'd be Gracie Basie Macy Tracy Lacy Spacey Casey.

If Ivana Trump married Mister Bean, then divorced him and married King Oscar of Norway, then divorced him and married Mike Myers, and then divorced him and married Anthony Wiener, she'd be Ivana Bean Oscar Myers Wiener.

Nog (Quark's brother on *Star Trek: Deep Space Nine*) has no other name, so he uses it twice when he gets a marriage license and takes the last name of his wife. If he married Finola Hughes, then divorced her and married Brynn Thayer, he'd be Nog Nog Hughes Thayer...which leads us into the next chapter.

Don't Knock Knock-Knock Jokes

More than four centuries ago, William Shakespeare, in his play *Macbeth,* quilled these lines for the Porter: "Knock, knock! Who's there, in the name of Beelzebub? Knock, knock!…Who's there, in the other devil's name?…Knock, knock, knock. Who's there? Never at quiet!"

It may be stretching a point to assert that Shakespeare invented the knock-knock joke, but the genre has been popular in the United States since the 1920s. Language author and historian Paul Dickson believes that "the knock-knock may be the first truly American formulaic form of humor," one that is baked into our folk culture.

Knock, knock.
Who's there?
Wooden shoe.
Wooden shoe who?
Wooden shoe like to hear a bunch of knock-knock jokes?

Knock, knock.
Who's there?
Boo!
Boo who?
Don't cry. You're about to laugh at some knock-knock jokes.

Knock, knock.
Who's there?

Hearsay.
Hearsay who?
Hearsay parade of knock-knock jokes.

Knock, knock.
Who's there?
Hair comb.
Hair comb who?
Hair comb a pack of knock-knock jokes.

Now, gaze upon a registry of knock-knock jokes that play upon first names. I provide only the *punc*h lines. You can supply the "Knock, knock. Who's There? _____. _____ who?" parts.

- *Adelle* is what a farmer lives in.
- *Amos* quito bit me.
- *Andy* bit me again.
- *Arthur* mometer is broken.
- *Barry* me not on the lone prairie.

- *Ben Hur* an hour and she hasn't shown up.
- *Della* catessen.
- *Desdemona* Lisa hanging on the wall.
- *Dexter* halls with boughs of holly.
- *Freda* prisoners.

- *Harry* up. We're late.
- *Henrietta* big dinner and got sick.
- *Ira* member Mama.
- *Isabel* out of order?
- *Isadore* locked?

- *Ivana* hold your hand.
- *José* can you see?

- *Keith* me, please.
- *Lionel* roar if you don't feed it.
- *Oliver* troubles will soon be over.

- *Oswald* my bubble gum.
- *Phillip* the tub so I can take a bath.
- *Sam and Janet* evening, you may see a stranger.
- *Sarah* doctor in the house?
- *Sherwood* like a cold drink.

- *Tarzan* stripes forever.
- *Walter* wall carpeting.
- *Wayne* dwops keep falling on my head.
- *Wendy* moon comes over the mountain.
- *Yoda* best knock-knock punster I've ever met!

Knock, knock.
Who's there?
Amsterdam.
Amsterdam who?
Amsterdam tired of these knock-knock jokes.

Knock, knock.
Who's there?
Consumption.
Consumption who?
Consumption be done to stop these ridiculous knock-knock jokes?

Knock, knock.
Who's there?
Celeste.
Celeste who?
Celeste time I tell you to knock it off!

Knock, knock.
Who's there?
Orange juice.
Orange juice who?
Orange juice glad that this'll be my very last knock-knock joke?

Grammar Stammers

Sir Winston hurled back at the editor a memorable rebuttal: " *This is the sort of arrant pedantry up which I will not put!* "

Best Grammar Laugh Lines

I am an officer for the Grammar Police. I pull people over and ticket them for Reckless Punctuation, Faulty Subject-Verb Agreement, Splitting Their Infinitives, Terminal Prepositions, Verb Tense Disorder, Misplacement of Modifiers, and Dangling Their Participles in Public.

On the side of my police car is emblazoned *Grammar Cops / To Serve and Correct.*

I used to correct my friends' grammar, too, but I stopped. That's because I decided it's better to have friends than to always be right. Nonetheless, I share my favorite quips about grammar, spelling, and punctuation.

My tolerance for incorrect pronunciation, grammar, punctuation, and spelling is extremely low these days. I used to have some immunity built up, but obviously there are new variants out there.

- It's not who you know. It's *whom* you know. Do not ask for who the bell tolls. It tolls for *whom.*
- Whenever one of my classroom students asked me, "Can I go to the bathroom?" I replied, "I sure hope so!"
- One of the most beloved of Rodgers and Hammerstein's musicals is being revived around the country — but its new title is *Me and the King.*
- An English teacher asked a student to name two pronouns. The student responded, "Who, me?"
- The auto-correct program is a tiny gremlin inside your computer who tries hard to be helpful but who is quite drunk. As

a result, auto-correct can become your worst enema. Turns out that the inventor of auto-correct has died. Her funnel will be held tomato.

- Saint Peter hears a knocking at the gates of Heaven and calls out, "Who's there?"

    "It is I," a voice responds.

    "Good," says Saint Peter. "That must be another English teacher. Come right in!"

- My wife was in labor with our first child. Things were going pretty well when suddenly she began shouting, "I'll! We're! Can't! Don't! Won't! Shouldn't! Wouldn't! Couldn't!"

    "Doctor, what's wrong with my wife?" I cried.

    "It's perfectly normal," he assured me. "She's having contractions."

- In the Julie Andrews-Dick Van Dyke film version of *Mary Poppins,* Bert the Chimney Sweep tells Uncle Albert, "I know a man with a wooden leg named Smith."

    "What's the name of the other leg?" Uncle Albert asks.

- What do you say to calm down a bad speller? "There, their, they're."

- I powerfully suspect that the person who decided how to spell *Wednesday* is the same person who put the first *r* in *February.*

- George Bernard Shaw, who bequeathed a sizable (also sizeable) sum of money to the cause of simplified spelling, announced that he had discovered a new way to spell the word *fish*. His fabrication turned out to be *ghoti: gh* as in rou*gh, o* as in w*o*men, and *ti* as in na*ti*on.

- First, they came for the adverbs, and I said nothing, even though I knew that this action did not bode good for our language.

    Then they came for the verbs, and I said nothing, even though I seen it coming and knew that good grammar had went away and verbing weirds our language.

Then they came for the pronouns, and me and my friends said nothing, even though we knew that pronoun case is important.

And then they came for I.

- Written quizzes about grammar have elicited creative grammar stammers from our budding scholars:

  Q. What are the parts of speech? *A.* The parts of speech are lungs and air.

  Q. What is a pronoun? *A.* A pronoun is a professional noun.

  Q. What is syntax? A. Syntax is all the money collected from the church from sinners.

  Q. Give an example of a collective noun. *A.* A vacuum cleaner.

  Q. An abstract noun is something you can think about but can't touch. Give an example of an abstract noun. *A.* My father's car.

50 Rules for Writing Good

Recently, scientists have discovered that a single dominant gene controls the ability to learn the rules of grammar. These days, more and more people are getting caught with their genes down and their shaky sentence structure exposed. These folks need to go back to Grammar School.

One of the popular items that circulate through the internet is a bubble-off-plumb set of rules along the lines of "Thimk," "We Never Make Misteaks," and "Plan Ahe…" — injunctions that call attention to the very mistakes they seek to enjoin. I've been collecting and making up these self-contradictions for decades and am pleased to share the best ones. Whatever you think of these cracked nuggets of rhetorical wisdom, just remember that all generalizations are bad.

1. Each pronoun should agree with their antecedent.
2. Between you and I, pronoun case is important.
3. A writer must be sure to avoid using sexist pronouns in his writing.
4. Verbs has to agree with their subjects.
5. Don't be a person whom people realize confuses *who* and *whom.*

6. Never use no double negatives.
7. Never use a preposition to end a sentence with.
8. When writing, participles must not be dangled.
9. Be careful to never, under any circumstances, split infinitives.
10. Hopefully, you won't float your adverbs.

11. A writer must not shift your point of view.
12. Lay down and die before using a transitive verb without an object.
13. Join clauses good, like a conjunction should.
14. The passive voice should be avoided.
15. About sentence fragments.

16. Don't verb nouns.
17. In letters themes reports and ad copy use commas to separate items in a series.
18. Don't use commas, that aren't necessary.
19. "Don't overuse 'quotation marks.'"
20. Parenthetical remarks (however relevant) are (if the truth be told) superfluous.

21. Contractions won't, don't, and can't help your writing voice.
22. Don't write run-on sentences they are hard to read.
23. Don't forget to use end punctuation
24. Its important to use apostrophe's in the right place's.
25. Don't abbrev.

26. Don't overuse exclamation marks!!!
27. Resist Unnecessary Capitalization.
28. Avoid mispellings.
29. Proofread carefully to see if you any words out.
30. One-word sentences? Never.

31. Avoid annoying, affected, and awkward alliteration, always.
32. When writing, never, ever use repetitive redundancies that are superfluous and not needed.
33. The bottom line is to bag trendy locutions that sound flaky.
34. By observing the distinctions between adjectives and adverbs, you will treat your readers real good.
35. Parallel structure will help you in writing more effective sentences and to express yourself more gracefully.

36. In my own personal opinion at this point of time, I think that authors, when they are writing, should not get into the habit of making use of too many unnecessary words that they don't really need.
37. Foreign-sounding words and phrases are the reader's bête noire and are not apropos.
38. Who needs rhetorical questions?
39. Don't count all your chickens in one basket.
40. Do not cast statements in the negative form.

41. So don't start sentences with coordinating conjunctions.
42. Avoid mixed metaphors. They will kindle a flood of confusion in your readers.
43. Eliminate quotations. As Ralph Waldo Emerson said, "I hate quotations. Tell me what you know."
44. Analogies in writing are like feathers on a snake.
45. Go around the barn at high noon to avoid colloquialisms.

46. Be more or less specific.
47. If I've told you once, I've told you a thousand times, exaggeration is a billion times worse than understatement, which is always best.
48. Never use a big word when you can utilize a diminutive word.
49. Profanity sucks.
50. Last but not least, bend over backward to avoid old-hat clichés like the plague.

TERMINAL PREPOSITIONS

In colleges and universities, students from time to time lead a cow upstairs and into an administrator's office. The prank is popular because while you can lead a cow upstairs, you can't lead it downstairs. I know a number of cows like this. They're the bogus usage rules that self-appointed grammarians herd into our national consciousness. It isn't long before we can't get them — the pundits and their rules — out.

One of the most widely circulated and totally phony grammar rules is "Never end a sentence with a preposition." The most famous story about the injunction against terminal prepositions involves Sir Winston Churchill, one of the greatest of all English prose stylists. As the story goes, an officious editor had the audacity to correct a proof of Churchill's memoirs by revising a sentence that ended with the outlawed preposition.

Sir Winston hurled back at the editor a memorable rebuttal: "This is the sort of arrant pedantry up with which I will not put!"

For the punster there's the setup joke about the prisoner who asks a female guard to marry him on the condition that she help him escape. This is a man attempting to use a proposition to end a sentence with.

Then there's the one about the little boy who has just gone to bed when his father comes into the room carrying a book about Australia. Surprised, the boy asks, "What did you bring that book that I didn't want to be read to out of from about Down Under up for?"

My favorite of all terminal preposition stories involves a boy attending public school and one attending private school who end up sitting next to each other in an airplane. To be friendly, the public schooler turns to the preppie and asks, "What school are you at?"

The preppy looks down his aquiline nose at the public-school student and comments, "I happen to attend an institution at which we are taught to know better than to conclude sentences with prepositions."

The public-school boy pauses for a moment and then says, "All right, then. What school are you at, a**hole!"

A Tense Time with Verbs

An English teacher spent a lot of time marking grammatical errors in her students' written work. She wasn't sure how much impact she was having until one overly busy day when she sat at her desk rubbing her temples.

A student asked, "What's the matter, Mrs. Bennett?"

"Tense," she replied, describing her emotional state.

After a slight pause, the student tried again. "What was the matter? What has been the matter? What will be the matter? What might have been the matter?"

Have you heard about the woman who asked a Boston cab driver where she could get scrod? "I didn't know that the verb had that past tense," muttered the cabbie.

Both jokes rely on the fact that verb tenses in English are crazy, fraught with a fearful asymmetry and puzzling unpredictability. Some verbs form their past tense by adding *-d, -ed,* or *-t—walk, walked; bend, bent.* Others go back in time through an internal vowel change — *begin, began; sing, sang.* Another cluster adds *-d* or *-t* and undergoes an internal vowel change — *lose, lost; buy, bought.* And still others don't change at all — *set, set; put, put.* No wonder, then, that our eyes glaze and our breath quickens when we have to form the past tense of verbs like *dive, weave, plead, shine,* and *sneak.*

The past tenses of verbs in our language cause so many of us to become tense that I've written a poem about the insanity:

Tense Verbs

The verbs in English are a fright.
How can we learn to read and write?
Today we speak, but first we spoke.
Some faucets leak, but never loke.
Today we write, but first we wrote.
We bite our tongues, but never bote.

Each day I teach; for years I've taught,
And preachers preach, but never praught.
This tale I tell; this tale I told.
I smell the flowers, but never smold.

If knights still slay, as once they slew,
Then do we play, as once we plew?
If I still do as once I did,
Then do cows moo, as they once mid?

I love to win, and games I've won.
I seldom sin, and never son.
I hate to lose, and games I've lost.
I didn't choose, and never chost.

I love to sing, and songs I sang.
I fling a ball, but never flang.
I strike that ball; that ball I struck.
This poem I like, but never luck.

I take a break; a break I took.
I bake a cake, but never book.
I eat that cake; that cake I ate.
I beat an egg, but never bate.

I often swim, as I once swam.
I skim some milk, but never skam.
I fly a kite that I once flew.
I tie a knot, but never tew.

I see the truth; the truth I saw.
I flee from falsehood, never flaw.
I stand for truth, as I once stood.
I land a fish, but never lood.

About these verbs I sit and think.
These verbs don't fit. They seem to wink
At me, who sat for years and thought
Of verbs that never fat or wought.

THE DEPARTMENT
OF REDUNDANCY DEPARTMENT

I am surrounded by an army of recurrently repetitive redundancies. In fact, I am completely surrounded. Even more than that, I am completely surrounded on all sides. These repeated redundancies are in close proximity to my immediate vicinity, which is a lot worse than their being in distant proximity in a vicinity far away.

I turn on the radio or television and learn that "at 10 a.m. in the morning" a man has been found "fatally slain," "leaving no living survivors," that three convicts "have successfully escaped" (how else does one do it?), that "foreign imports" are threatening to destroy the balance of trade (by outnumbering the domestic imports, presumably), that the weather is "minus ten degrees below zero."

Sports announcers inform me that a certain fullback has had his "forward progress stopped," that a promising young athlete "has a fine future ahead of him" (while my athletic future is long behind me), and that a track star has just set a "new record," a feat much more newsworthy than setting an old record.

I am adrift in a sea of American overspeak. The sea is a perfectly appropriate metaphor here, for the word *redundancy* is a combination of the Latin *undare,* "to overflow" and *re-,* "back."

Richard Nixon eulogized the life of statesman Adlai Stevenson with these words: "In eloquence of expression he had no peers and few equals." Peers are not superiors; they *are* equals.

Other gems of political overspeak uttered by head honchos (who are higher up than subordinate honchos) include "I'm in favor of letting the status quo stay as it is," "I'm going to proceed ahead. Someone has to do it," and "In the 1930s, we were not just a nation on our backs. We were prone on our backs." I assure you that these examples are all true facts.

The pervasive and persuasive messages of advertising are fraught with false pretenses, which are a lot more dangerous than true pretenses. One stack of products is "100 percent pure," certainly more pristine than being 50 percent pure. Other product boxes trumpet the arrival of a "new and improved bold, new innovation," which sure beats any bold, old innovation. I do wonder if something can really be both new *and* improved.

McDonald's hamburger emporia boast of "Billions and Billions Sold." Is billions and billions any more than mere billions? Raid insecticide "kills bugs dead," which is just the way they should be killed.

Save 40% off!" blares the typical special-sale sign. Strip joints advertise "Totally, totally nude! Live girls," much more entertaining than partially nude dead girls. Various hotels promise "a honeymoon for two" — the old fashioned kind! Of all the adspeak that congests my mailbox the one I most hate with a passion (rather than calmly hating it) is "free gift." Sometimes I am even offered a "complimentary free gift." I sigh with relief, grateful that I won't have to pay for that gift.

My fellow colleagues and classmates, I am here to tell you the honest truth, not to be confused with the dishonest truth, about the basic fundamentals of (aren't all fundamentals fundamentally basic?) redundancies. My past experience, which is a lot more reliable than my present or future experience, tells me that overspeak will not go away. The past history of redundancies gives us but a small inkling (can an inkling ever be large?) of the repeats that will fill our future history. Embedded in the idea of experience and history is the past, yet we persist in talking about someone's past experience and past history. Plans and warnings, in contrast, are by definition futuristic, yet every day we hear about future plans, advance warnings, and forewarnings.

Simple initials generate letter-imperfect redundancies — *ABM missile, AC current, CNN network, PIN number, ISBN number, VIN number, HIV virus, OPEC country, SALT talks* (or *treaty*), and *SAT test*. In each of these initialisms, the last letter is piled on by a superfluous noun. *ATM machine* is a double redundancy: *Machine* repeats the *M*, and the *M* repeats *the A*. A machine, by definition, *is* automated. If you agree with my observation, RSVP please.

Then there's "at this point in time." Either "at this point" or "at this time" will do just fine, and "now" is even better. "At this point in time" is the bureaucrat's way of spelling "now" by using 17 letters. This atrocity elicits from this old geezer (I confess that I am no longer a young geezer) an audible (louder than an inaudible) groan, exacerbates all my aches and pains, and sets me not just to ranting or to raving, but to ranting and raving. I am not just bound or just determined but bound and determined to stamp out the last vestige, rather than the first vestige, of this classic example of logorrhea and declare it not just null or just void, but null and void. May all of us cease and desist using "at this point in time."

I don't understand the whys and wherefores of various and sundry twosomes, in which the two halves (certainly not three or more halves) are for all intents and purposes one and the same. Caught betwixt and between such examples of linguistic conspicuous consumption, I'll pick and choose a few more of these hard and fast doublets, which are anything but fine and dandy, tip top, well and good, hale and hearty, fair and just, and spick and span.

Redundancies are the junk food of our language. Alas and alack, when we gorge on their empty calories, we accumulate adipose tissue in the nooks and crannies of our waist-lines in dribs and drabs and bits and pieces — and I challenge you to tell me the differences between alas and alack, a nook and a cranny, a drib and a drab, and a bit and a piece. Indeed, in this day and age, redundancies are multiplying by fits and starts and leaps and bounds. Rather than aiding and abetting these fattening snack-size doublets, let us find the ways and means to oppose them with all our vim and vigor and might and main. Lo and behold, perhaps one day they will be over and done with and we shall be free and clear of them in a safe haven (but aren't all havens by definition safe?).

Can we ever cure ourselves of our national addiction to fatty and fattening redundancies that ooze into our parlance anywhere and everywhere, over and over, and again and again? I hope it won't come as an unexpected surprise (rather than a surprise you expected) that I believe that we can. As the old adage goes, "If at first you don't succeed, try, try again." Of course, by their very nature adages are old. That is how they get to be adages.

The sum total and end result (about as final as you can get) is that we can join together (more effective than joining apart) to fight the good fight against every single one of these redundancies. We can drive them from our house and home. We can bring them, in the words of many a flight attendant, to a complete stop, and we can kill them dead. That would be so incredible it would be unbelievable.

I Before *E*, Except ...

The most famous of mnemonic spelling jingles advises the
following:

I before *e*,
Except after *c*,
Unless sounded as *a*,
As in *neighbor* and *weigh*.

A popular mug reads "I BEFORE E except when your foreign
neighbor Keith receives eight counterfeit beige sleighs from feisty
caffeinated weightlifters."

As Albert Einstein once wrote, "*I* before *e*, except after *c*? That's
just weird science."

You don't have to be an Einstein to realize that the *i*-before-*e*
rule is breached as often as it is observed. If you want to find out
just how many proper names violate the rule, remember this sentence: "Eugene *O'Neil* and Dwight *Eisenhower* drank a 35° *Fahrenheit
Budweiser* and *Rheingold* in *Anaheim* and *Leicester*." You also don't
have to be an Einstein to see that *Einstein* itself is a double violation
of the *i*-before-*e* rule (along with *Weinstein, Feinstein, deficiencies, effi-
ciencies, proficiencies,* and *zeitgeist*).

In addition to the previously described mug, in which *e* pre-
cedes *i*, are the likes of *atheist, either, heifer, height, heist, herein, leisure,
protein, reign, rein, seize,* and *veil*.

And among words in which *c* is immediately followed by *ie*, we note *ancient, concierge, conscience, fancier, financier, glacier, omniscient, science, society, species, sufficient,* and *tendencies.*

To show how much this rule was made to be broken, I offer a poem of mine that I hope will leave you spellbound:

E-I, I-E — Oh?

There's a rule that's sufficient, proficeint, efficeint.
For all speceis of spelling in no way deficeint.
While the glaceirs of ignorance icily frown,
This soveriegn rule warms, like a thick iederdown.

On words fiesty and wierd it shines from great hieghts,
Blazes out like a beacon, or skien of ieght lights.
It gives nieghborly guidance, sceintific and fair,
To this nonpariel language to which we are hier.

Now, a few in soceity fiegn to deride
And to forfiet thier anceint and omnisceint guide,
Diegn to worship a diety foriegn and hienous,
Whose counterfiet riegn is certain to pain us.

In our work and our liesure, our agenceis, schools,
Let us all wiegh our consceince, sieze proudly our rules.
It's plebiean to lower our standards. I'll niether
Give in or give up — and I trust you won't iether!

ON YOUR MARKS!

I just had a consultation with my physician. She said, "Don't eat anything fatty."

I asked her, "Do you mean things like hamburgers and bacon?"

"No," she said, "I meant 'Fatty, don't eat anything!'"

Punctuation matters. To discover how a slight difference in punctuation can make a vast difference in meaning, examine each pair of sentences, and choose the one that answers the question correctly:

1. Which employee should be fired?
   a. The butler stood at the door and called the guests names.
   b. The butler stood at the door and called the guests' names.

2. Which situation is worse for the Democratic Party?
   a. Democrats who are seen as weak will not be elected.
   b. Democrats, who are seen as weak, will not be elected.

3. Which scene is more threatening?
   a. I saw a man-eating lobster.
   b. I saw a man eating lobster.

4. Which speaker is Ishmael's girlfriend?
   a. Call me Ishmael.
   b. Call me, Ishmael.

5. Which speaker is a cannibal?
   a. Let's eat Grandma.
   b. Let's eat, Grandma.

6. Which of the following book dedications is correct?
   a. To my parents, the Pope and Mother Teresa
   b. To my parents, the Pope, and Mother Teresa

Answers

1. *a*   2. *b*   3. *a*   4. *b*   5. *a*   6. *b*

- My three favorite things are eating my family and not using commas.
- What's the difference between a cat and a comma? A cat has claws at the end of its paws. A comma is a pause at the end of a clause.
- A school principal came into a teacher's classroom and said she was spending too much time teaching about commas because they weren't all that important in communicating content. So the teacher had a student write the sentence "The principal says the teacher is wrong" on the board and then asked the principal to put a comma after the word *principal* and another after the word *teacher.* The result, of course, was "The principal, says the teacher, is wrong."
- Have a look at the two love notes below. The words are the same in both versions, but see how punctuation can make the difference between a second date and a restraining order.

Dear Mary,
The dinner we shared the other night — it was absolutely lovely!
Not in my wildest dreams could I ever imagine anyone as perfect as
you are. Could you — if only for a moment — think of our being
together forever? What a cruel joke to have you come into my life only
to leave again. It would be heaven denied. The possibility of seeing
you again makes me giddy with joy. I face the time we are apart with
great sadness. I would like to tell you that I love you. I can't stop
thinking that you are one of the prettiest women on earth. Please let
me be yours.

John

Dear Mary,
The dinner we shared the other night. It was absolutely lovely — not!
In my wildest dreams, could I ever imagine anyone? As perfect as
you are, could you — if only for a moment — think? Of our being
together forever, what a cruel joke! To have you come into my life
only to leave again — it would be heaven! Denied the possibility of
seeing you again makes me giddy. With joy, I face the time we are
apart. With great sadness, I would like to tell you that I love you. I
can't. Stop thinking that you are one of the prettiest women on earth.
Please let me be.

Yours
John

HILARIOUS HOLIDAY HUMOR

Titanic, gigantic Godzilla
Stomped on Tokyo, then on Manila.
Then sank a flotilla,
Then fought a gorilla,
And wasn't ashamed one scintilla!

NEW YEAR'S IRRESOLUTIONS

The passing of one year into the beginning of another is marked around the world by New Year's Eve customs ranging from high-spirited parties to solemn prayer and thought. The biggest and most famous New Year's party takes place in New York City. Millions of people around the world watch the ginormous Waterford Crystal Ball drop over Times Square.

"Auld Lang Syne," written by the Scottish poet Robert Burns, is the song most identified with New Year's celebrations. Almost all of us can sing "Auld Lang Syne," but few of us really know what it means, which happens to be "old long since." The song was first popularized in 1929 by Guy Lombardo and His Royal Canadians orchestra.

We make New Year's resolutions, vowing to better ourselves in the coming year. But most of these resolutions go in one year and out the other and are forgotten shortly after they're made. In fact, roughly 80 percent of all New Year's resolutions are broken by the end of February.

I believe that taking a few moments to reflect on our short-comings and optimistically plan to overcome them is better than making no attempt at all. And sometimes, when we are ready for change, those resolutions do stick — some for a lifetime.

When they drop the ball in Times Square on New Year's Eve, it's a reminder of what I did all last year. So, for this year,

- I resolve not to drop the ball.
- I resolve to get better at pretending to know the words to "Auld Lang Syne."

- I was going to quit all my bad habits, but I realized that nobody likes a quitter.
- I resolve to take all the Christmas lights down by Easter.

- I resolve to get in shape. Round is a shape.
- I resolve to get more exercise, so I've moved the refrigerator into the basement.
- I resolve to lose weight by inventing an anti-gravity machine. If that doesn't work, I resolve to help all my friends gain 10 pounds so I look skinnier.
- I resolve to read more, so I'm going to put the captions up on my TV screen.

- I resolve to leave the toilet seat down, as long as my wife promises to leave the toilet seat up.
- I resolve to get better at multitasking, so I'm going to start texting while sitting on the toilet.
- I resolve to stop making the same mistake twice. Instead, I'll make a different mistake each time.
- I resolve to stop messing up my online passwords, so I've changed all of them to "incorrect." Now, every time I key in the wrong code, the computer reminds me that "Your password is incorrect."

- I resolve to be more positive and less sarcastic. Yeah, sure.
- I resolve to take criticism better, so don't contradict me.
- I resolve to stop putting my foot in my mouth, and I bet you resolve to lose weight. Right?
- I resolve to stop letting my mood swings control my life. Nah, I'm not up for that.

- I resolve to conserve water by taking fewer showers and baths.
- I resolve to floss every day, and not just with wild abandon the day before my dental cleaning.

- I resolve to stop repeating myself again and again and again.
- I resolve to stop repeating myself again and again and again.

- I resolve to stop hanging out with people who ask me about my New Year's resolutions.
- I resolve to acquire all leftover 2020, 2021, and 2022 calendars and burn them.
- I resolve to live forever. So far, so good. If I fail to keep this resolution, I will die trying.
- I resolve to break all my New Year's resolutions. That way I can succeed at something.

As your reader-friendly Attila the pun, my final Gnu Year's resolution is to tell ewe a gazelleon times how much I caribou ewe, deer. I'm a wildebeest of a punster, and you're thinking, "Unicorniest fellow I've ever met!" but I'm not out to buffalo or a llama ewe, so alpaca bag and hightail it out of here in camelflage.

May all your troubles last as long as the success of your New Year's resolutions!

WHEN IRISH WORDS ARE SMILING

St. Patrick is the patron saint of Ireland. Legend has it that he drove the snakes out of Ireland, although in fact snakes were never there. The legend may be referring to Patrick's expelling the Druidic religion and bringing Christianity to the Emerald Isle. Patrick died on March 17, A.D. 460, and the Catholic Church made that his saint's day. As a result, March 17 is the date of St. Patrick's Day each year.

In the United States, more than 30 million people claim at least some Irish heritage. Many cities host annual St. Patrick's Day parades in which Irish pride is on display. The city of Chicago even adds a temporary dye to the Chicago River to turn it green for a day.

Knock, knock.
Who's there?
Irish.
Irish who?
Irish you a happy St. Patrick's Day.

To err is human, to share humor, bovine. So here I am throwing some bull — not just any bull, but an Irish bull. And while I'm at it, I'll round up a herd of Irish bulls.

What's an Irish bull? I'm glad I asked me that. Some dismiss it as a silly blunder born on the Emerald Isle. Others describe an Irish bull as a statement fueled by a delightful absurdity that sparks forth a memorable truth, such as Oscar Wilde's spot-on "I can resist anything but temptation."

When asked the difference between an Irish bull and any other kind of bull, Professor John Pentland Mahaffey of Dublin University replied, "An Irish bull is always pregnant," providing a definition that is itself an example.

Among the first and most famous specimens is a pronouncement by eighteenth century politician Sir Boyle Roche, who once asked, "Why should we do anything to put ourselves out of the way for posterity? What has posterity ever done for us?" Irish politics, literature, and folklore are replete with pronouncements that jump to a confusion:

An Irishman is never at peace except when he's fighting.

An Irishman will die before letting himself be buried outside of Ireland.

I'd give my right arm to be ambidextrous.

Your Honor, I was sober enough to know I was drunk.

Gentleman, it appears to be unanimous that we cannot agree.

Half the lies our opponents tell about us are not true.

Thank God I'm an atheist.

God bless the Holy Trinity.

May you never live to see your wife a widow.

This piece is chock full of omissions.

He is the kind of opponent who would stab you in front of your face and then stab you in the chest when your back is turned.

Any assumptions that the Irish have cornered the bull market are completely unwarranted. Some of the best specimens of taurine eloquence thrive far from the green fields of Ireland. Jazz pianist and composer Eubie Blake, who lived to the age of 96, began smoking at six and refused to drink water. He observed, "If I had known I was going to live this long, I'd have taken better care of myself."

Now gaze upon some more examples of corn-fed American bulls:

Always go to other people's funerals. Otherwise, they won't come to yours. *-Yogi Berra*

Good pitching always stops good hitting, and vice versa. *-Casey Stengel*

I am free of all prejudice. I hate everybody equally. *—W.C. Fields*

Please accept my resignation. I don't want to belong to any club that will have me as a member *-Groucho Marx*

It's not that I'm afraid to die. I just don't want to be there when it happens. *-Woody Allen*

Anybody who goes to a psychiatrist ought to have his head examined. *-Samuel Goldwyn*

Always be sincere, even if you don't mean it. *-President Harry S. Truman*

This is why the sagacious Hobbes, the insightful tiger who prowled Bill Waterston's late lamented comic strip *Calvin and Hobbes,* once predicted. "We can eventually make language a complete impediment to everything."

Nothing Works for Me

In North America, Labor Day falls on the first Monday in September. These days, Labor Day is largely a time for family togetherness and relaxation. Cookouts and leisure activities such as boating, fishing, camping, and picnicking are popular ways to spend the Labor Day weekend as people seek to enjoy take advantage of the summer sunshine before autumn sets in.

In honor of Labor Day, I share with you my personal workplace history. Some people hold the same job for their entire career. Others move from one job to another while relentlessly ascending the corporate ladder. My career is more checkered.

My first job was working in an orange juice factory, but I couldn't concentrate, so I got canned. Then I became a lumberjack, but I just couldn't hack it, so they gave me the axe. I was once a set designer, but I left without making a scene. I was next employed at a diet center, but I got downsized. I became a baker, but I turned out to be a loafer and couldn't make enough dough.

Then I opened a donut shop, but I soon got fed up with the hole business. For a while, I manufactured calendars, but my days were numbered, and they fired me when I took a day off. After that, I tried to be a tailor, but I just wasn't suited for it, because it was a sew-sew job, depleating and depressing. I took a job as an upholsterer, but I never recovered.

Next, I worked in a muffler factory, but that was exhausting. I became a hairdresser, but the job was just too cut-and-dried. I moved on to selling lingerie, but they decided to give me a pink slip. I tried telemarketing, but I had too many hang-ups. I manned a computer but developed a terminal illness and lost my drive and my memory.

I became a dentist, but gummed up the works and couldn't do the drill. The job was boring and felt like a bridge to nowhere. I tried selling vacuum cleaners, but I abhor a vacuum, and the job really sucked. I worked as a fortune-teller, but I didn't see any future in it. I studied a long time to become a doctor, but I didn't have the patients. I sold origami, but the business folded.

I became a Velcro salesman but couldn't stick with it. For a while, I was an astrologer, but it wasn't in the stars. Then I tried to be a chef. I figured it would add a little spice to my life, but I just didn't have the thyme, it didn't pan out, and my goose was cooked. I attempted to be a deli worker, but any way I sliced it, I couldn't cut the mustard.

I became a cardiologist, but my heart just wasn't in it. I took a job at UPS, but I couldn't express myself. Next came work in a shoe factory, but the job didn't last and I got the boot. I studied to become a lawyer, but my career was brief. It was too trying and had no appeal. I tried being a teacher, but I soon lost my principal, my faculties, and my class.

Just for the halibut, I was a commercial fisherman, but I missed the boat and discovered that I couldn't tackle the job and live on my net income. I tried being a masseur, but I rubbed people the wrong way. I was once a photographer, but I never developed. It was a negative experience, and I hated the hot flashes. I became a Hawaiian garland maker, but I got leid off. I became a professional yo-yoer. I went around the world, but the job had too many strings attached.

I was a printer for a while, but I wasn't the type for the job, and I didn't have an inkling about what to do. I tried being a fireman, but I suffered burnout, so I couldn't climb my way to the top. I got a job at a zoo feeding giraffes, but I was fired because I wasn't up to it. I wanted to be a banker, but I wasn't ready to make a change. I lacked interest and maturity. One day a lady asked me to check her balance, so I pushed her over.

So then I became a personal trainer in a gym, but they said I wasn't fit for the job. I tried selling cigarette lighters, but I lost my spark. Next, I found being an electrician interesting, but I had to strip to make ends meet. I wasn't emotionally grounded and the work was shocking and revolting, so they discharged me. I applied for a job at an Air & Space Museum, but there was nothing inside.

I thought that becoming a tennis pro would yield a net gain, but it wasn't my kind of racket. I was too high-strung and didn't have any love for the game. I trained to be a ballet dancer, but I was seldom on point and it was tutu difficult. For a while, I was a farmer, but problems cropped up and I wasn't outstanding in my field.

I took the plunge as a plumber, but it turned out to be a pipe dream. I was out of sync, so the job went down the drain. I worked as an elevator operator. The job had its ups and downs. I got the shaft and took steps to quit. I thought about becoming a poet, but the work was a verse to my being. Iamb what iamb.

I sold chocolate ice cream with diced marshmallows and nuts, but the job turned out to be a rocky road. I became a candle maker. At first, business waxed strong. Then it tapered off. My first day on the snow job as a ski instructor I slipped up, and it was all downhill from there. I did a stint in a pizza shop. I kneaded the dough, but my pies were too cheesy.

I took a job as a cook in a monastery as both the fish friar and the chip monk. I tried to communicate with the clergy, but they excommunicated me. I once worked as an optometrist. The future looked clear, and my life was coming into focus. Then I got too close to the lens grinder and made a spectacle of myself. I tried cleaning pools, but I was out of my depth.

I became a statistician, but I got broken down by age, sex, and marital status. I was once a Scrabble champion, but I became inconsonant, and I can't move my vowels anymore. My next trip to the bathroom could spell disaster!

So I've retired, and I find that I'm perfect for this job!

My Favorite
Halloween Monsters

What would you do if you opened your front door and saw Dracula, Frankenstein, a ghost, a ghoul, a mummy, a skeleton, a werewolf, a witch, and a zombie standing on your steps?

Hope it's Halloween.

Halloween is the year's spookiest holiday. On October 31, we carve glowering faces on pumpkins, put on scary costumes, take our children trick-or-treating, and devour mouth-watering, calorie-laden goodies, which always go to waist. Only on Halloween do parents encourage their kids to trespass on someone's property, make a nonnegotiable demand, and take candy from strangers. One quarter of all the candy sold annually in the United States is purchased for Halloween. Chocolate, which in itself is a major food group, is by far the most popular confection, followed by candy corn.

Human beings are fascinated by shambling monsters. We are drawn somehow to their ugliness. Monsters are appalling, freaky, ghastly, grotesque, gruesome, hair-raising, hideous, horrifying, repulsive, terrifying, and downright yucky creatures. They are so ugly that when they look in a mirror, their reflection looks back and screams. They are so ugly that even their own shadows run away from them. They are so ugly that the females enter ugly contests.

Don't You Dare

Don't ever play Ping-Pong with King Kong.
Don't ever take blood tests with Dracula.
Don't you dare give a wedgie to Frankenstein.
Your ending will be quite spectaculah!

Don't you dare snap a towel at Godzilla.
Such a prank would be foolishly rude.
Don't you dare floss the teeth of a werewolf.
You are liable to end up as food!

Don't you dare give a hotfoot to Bigfoot.
Don't point a stake at a vampire.
Don't you dare roast marshmallows with dragons.
You'll find you are playing with fire!

Don't you steal witches' brooms for spring cleaning.
Don't ever try scaring a ghost.
Don't ever eat breakfast with zombies.
You'll certainly end up on toast!

The Witches' Cauldron

Double, double, toil and trouble.
Fire burn and cauldron bubble.
Eye of Cyclops, werewolf's claw.
Skeleton's teeth and King Kong's paw.
Horseman's head and Hulk's green thumb.
Marinate in ghoul drool scum.
Dragon scales and zombie's ears.
Add a vial of ghostly tears.
Mummy's rags and wing of bat.
Tail of warty witch's cat.
Vampire's fang and Bigfoot's fur.
Give the yucky mix a stir!

I will eat it all with glee —
If it has no broccoli!
I'll swallow all, with happy shouts —
As long as there's no Brussels sprouts!

Now let's go out on a limerick, a highly disciplined exercise in light verse that is the most popular fixed poetic form indigenous to the English language. While other basic forms of poetry, such as the haiku, sonnet, and ode, are borrowed from other countries, the limerick is an original English language creation.

The limerick packs laughs anatomical
Into space that is quite economical.
But the good ones I've seen
So seldom are clean,
And the clean ones so seldom are comical.
-Vivyan Holland

Despite the opinion expressed in Holland's limerick about limericks, even the clean ones can be comical. Within the brief compass of five lines, the ditty can tell an engaging story or make a humorous statement compactly and cleverly.

For some unaccountable reason, I love writing limericks about funny Halloween monsters. Here — for your gratification, edification, and trepidation — I alphabetically unchain a fright of shambling monsterpieces that I've conjured up::

The **Abominable Snowman** is sweet.
Other monsters he knows how to treat.
He gave Sasquatch one shoe,
E width, size twenty-two,
'Cause Sasquatch is Bigfoot, not Bigfeet.

163

On a blind date, two **Cyclopes** said, "Hi."
"You're the one eye adore," they did sigh.
Now they're married for years,
And the secret appears
To be that they see eye to eye!

You're a woman from East Transylvania
Dating **Dracula**, with his weird mania.
He asks you each night
To go out for a bite —
An experience certain to drain ya!

A **dragon** with fiery plume
Crashed a wedding and smashed up the room.
Ate every hors d'oeuvre.
Crushed the cake. What a nerve!
Then toasted the bride and the groom!

Frankenstein sat on a wall.
Frankenstein had a great fall.
All the king's men
Could not sew back again
The body parts jointly at all!

Those **ghosts** — Hip, hooray! Hallelujah!
If you're famous, they're bound to pursue ya.
But here's advice sage:
If you sing on their stage,
The audience surely will boo ya!

Titanic, gigantic **Godzilla**
Stomped on Tokyo, then on Manila.
Then sank a flotilla,
Then fought a gorilla,
And wasn't ashamed one scintilla!

The **Hulk** wasn't very compliant.
He was mad and annoyed and defiant.
But he happened to pass
Anger management class —
And turned into The Jolly Green Giant!

The **Invisible Man** came to dine.
He sat right to my left, which was fine.
But his rumblings abdominal
Were simply phenomenal —
And everyone thought they were mine!

A monster that took many dips
In **Loch Ness** grew so wide in the hips.
It was her seafood diet:
She would see food, then try it.
She especially liked fish and ships!

A **mummy** who thought she was dying
Kept crying and crying and crying.
Until a ghoul said,
"You're already dead!"
Then that poor mummy's tears started drying.

A bell ringer named **Quasimodo**
Was abused by a hobbit named Frodo.
"Your back, it's a blob! It
Is gross!" said the hobbit.
Now that's how to act like a dodo!

A **skeleton** named Marguerite
Offered a toast quite upbeat.
Raised her mug with great pride,
Filled with formaldehyde,
And shouted out, "Bone appétit!"

A well-mannered **vampire** from Wheeling
Was endowed with such delicate feeling.
When he read on the door
"Don't spit on the floor,"
He flew up and then spat on the ceiling!

This limerick isn't a stretch.
It's about an unfortunate wretch.
A **werewolf** pursued him.
How did he elude him?
He threw it a stick and yelled, "Fetch!"

A **witch** burnt her butt on a candle.
She was angry. It was such a scandal.
She jumped on her broom
And zoomed to her doom.
Went too fast, so she flew off the handle!

An innocent fellow named Tim
Met a **zombie** quite horrid and grim.
Tim patted its head
Before it had fed.
I wonder what happened to him.

ALL ABOUT SANTA CLAUS

Christmas is the time of year when people exchange hellos and good buys with each other and when mothers have to separate the men from the toys. Christmas is a joyous occasion illuminated by candles and graced by decorations, ornamented Christmas trees, poinsettias, traditional songs and carols, church services, family feasts, the exchange of gifts and greeting cards, and the donning of ugly sweaters. Celebrants eagerly wait for the arrival of Santa Claus — also known as simply Saint Nicholas, Kriss Kringle, Father Christmas, simply Santa, or, in my fevered brain, The Abdominal Snowman.

Did you know that Santa's first language is North Polish? Santa and Mrs. Claus live in an icicle built for two. He lovingly tends his garden, all the while laughing, "Hoe, hoe, hoe!"

Santa always wears the same suit, but it stays clean because Mrs. Claus washes it in Yule Tide. Part of that suit is a black belt, which Santa earned in karate. But no matter how much he works out, Saint Nick suffers from a number of health problems, including mistle toe, tinselitis, and hollytosis.

You'll also discover that Santa is the main Claus. His wife is a relative Claus. His children are dependent Clauses. As a group, they're all renoun Clauses. And the father of Father Christmas is, of course, a Grandfather Claus.

Santa's elves are subordinate Clauses. They're generous souls, not elfish. They study the elf-abet so that they can file correctly, but like all staff, they do all the work, and the fat guy in the suit gets all the credit.

As they make toys, the elves sing, "Love Me Tender." That's why they're known as Santa's little Elvis. As they put the toys in boxes and prepare them for Santa's sack, they listen to wrap music. They also take a lot of elfies.

On Christmas Eve, Santa eats a jolly roll and leaps into his Holly-Davidson sleigh, and the toys hop into the sack. Santa's sleigh always comes out first because it starts in the Pole position. It also gets terrific mileage because it has long-distance runners on each side.

Santa especially loves all his reindeer because every buck is deer to him. He puts bells on all his reindeer because their horns don't work. On the way to delivering gifts, he lets his coursers stop at the Deery Queen. Dasher and Dancer love washing their meals down with coffee because they are Santa's star bucks. Santa's own favorite food is Crisp Pringles.

Santa has the right idea: Deliver your products free because they're on the house. The fact that Santa works just one day a year is an inspiration to workers everywhere, but also explains why he gets paid only with cookies and milk.

When traveling in the sleigh in inclement weather, Santa gets icicles in his beard. Real chin chillas, those. He sometimes removes all the bells from his sleigh and travels silently through the night. One day, he hopes to win a No Bell prize.

What's red and white and black all over? Santa Claus entering a home through a chimney. He loves sliding down chimneys because it soots him. But he actually has a fear of getting stuck. That fear is called Santa Claustrophobia. When Santa falls down a chimney, he becomes Santa Klutz. Since Santa has to go up and down a wide variety of chimneys on Christmas, he gets a yearly flue shot.

Whatever the obstacles, Santa always delivers his presents in the Saint Nick of time. Then on December 25, Santa is a beat Nick.

All I need to know I learned from Santa Claus:

- It's as much fun to give as it is to receive.
- Make your presents known.
- True joy comes from making children happy.
- Real estate is cheap in the North Pole.
- Be joyful and reliable, and people will believe in you.

- It's better to be nice than naughty.
- You better not pout. You better not cry.
- Surround yourself with a great team.
- Provide honest employment to others, including elves and reindeer.
- Honor diversity in your staff, like Rudolph's red nose, which led the way.

- Feel free to ask for what you want.
- Chubby is okay.
- Beards and moustaches are in.
- Bright red can make anyone look good.
- Wearing a wide, black belt will make you look slimmer.

- If you come to town only once a year, people will think you're important.
- Be thankful for kindness, especially when people leave you cookies and milk.
- Organize your data by making lists and checking them twice.
- If you laugh "Ho, Ho, Ho!" the world will laugh with you.
- Do what you love, and love what you do.

There are the five stages of a man's life:

(1) He believes in Santa Claus.
(2) He doesn't believe in Santa Claus.
(3) He dresses up to look like Santa Claus.
(4) He looks like Santa Claus.
(5) He believes he's Santa Claus.

Author Biography

Richard Lederer is the author of more than 50 books about language, history, and humor, including his best-selling *Anguished English* series and his current titles, *The Gift of Age, A Treasury of Halloween Humor, A Treasury of Christmas Humor, Richard Lederer's Ultimate Book of Literary Trivia,* and *The Complete Pleasury of Word & Phrase Origins.* He is a founding co-host of *A Way With Words,* broadcast on Public Radio.

Dr. Lederer's column, *Lederer on Language,* appears in newspapers and magazines throughout the United States. He has been named International Punster of the Year and Toastmasters International's Golden Gavel winner.

He lives in San Diego with his wife, Simone van Egeren.

richardhlederer@gmail.com / verbivore.com

Portrait of the Artist

Todd Smith has a long history of creating award-winning graphic design, photography, and illustrations. He has worked as an art director for a number of corporations and ad agencies and has created his own graphic design studio, focusing on design, photography, and illustrations, a number of them for Richard Lederer's books.

Todd lives with his wife Debbie in Asheville, North Carolina, where they own and operate a greeting card company (masalacards.com) based on the work of regional artists.

https://toddsmit2.wixsite.com/toddsportfolio/home

Made in the USA
Columbia, SC
02 November 2022

70336378R00104